Creative Against All Odds
Some Good Advice for Black Creatives

Written by
Michael Todd Thomas Jr.

For information contact :
For bulk ordering of book at a discount price please contact.
June Sun Publishing House a Kreadiv & Koo LLC Company
www.junesun.com

Booking Information:
miketodd@kreadivkoo.com

Book and Cover design by Michael Todd Thomas Jr.
ISBN-13: 978-0-578-47379-6

First Edition: April 2019
1

Every possible effort has been made to ensure that the information in this book is accurate at the time of the first publishing. The editor, publisher, or author cannot accept responsibility for damage or loss occasioned to any person acting or refraining from action as a result of the content of this production.

CONTENTS

I dedicate this book to you. I know how it feels to wake up every day wanting to paint what you dreamt of despite not having the paint brush to do so. I understand the frustration of pursuing your passion. I was just like you. All of the knowledge I have obtained has been self-taught through trial and error, and I believe it can be easily implemented. I genuinely want to see you succeed and hope you find help in my raw and unpolished approach to creative entrepreneurship.

Blessings, Michael Todd Thomas Jr.

1

Let's get the inspiration
out of the way

Chapter 1

"Success is not some microwaveable TV dinner. It's more like a slow cooked pot roast..."

Before we get down to the matter at hand, I have a few disclaimers. One, this book is not meant to inspire, although it might, this books sole purpose is meant to give you actionable information that can possible put you a better position to achieve your goals. To be honest if you're Black in America, look around or turn on the news and that should be enough inspiration. I just don't think you need another book screaming you have untapped potential, or another rich person telling you how to make money with no money. I'm not here to tell you that I was once in your shoes, nor I'm I here to encourage you to follow your dreams. Because odds are if you're taking the time out of your day to read this book you're probably already inspired enough.

Two, I am not an expert in black creativity; that's like saying I know what all black creatives go through. However, I am an expert in my black experience as a creative. As a creative person of color we face challenges that our counterparts don't, I want to shine some light some those issues that I have faced.

Three, this book won't make you rich, as matter of fact any book that claims that should be burned immediately. Although I have been able to make a decent living off my God-given creative talent money is not my motivation. Four, none of the advice or information you read in this book will help, if you don't get off your ass and actually do it. You will have to an immense amount of execution in order for anything you read in this book to work. That means you will have to trim some fat in your life. Five, since the people reading this book are not all the same, I don't expect all the information to resonate with everyone in the same way. Therefore, feel free to jump to the section you feel is necessary to you.

Overall, this book was created with the sole purpose of helping creatives of color; in particular, black creatives who want to accomplish career or entrepreneurial goals. If what's in these pages does not do that, you can always use the book as a coffee table decoration. The cover is dope!

Grandpa's creativity

I have always been a creative person. Seriously, I really have! I remember taking apart old VCRs just to see if I could put them back together or drawing cartoons like Dragon Ball Z when I saw them on TV. My dad's father, grandpa Robert Moore, first intrigued my creativity as when I was five years old. With no background in architecture, he'd build little log cabin models out of newspaper and Popsicle sticks. It wasn't a trade. It was something he learned in prison in the 80's. At that young impressionable age, I was in awe of his steady hands as they gracefully mollified materials that would be obsolete on any other day. The dude literally took items that people would normally throw away and made them into art. He was also a very good painter. One of his most memorable paintings was the depiction of a red barn resting on a heavy autumn day. The colors in that painting where so vivid, if you were to put it in a line-up with a hundred similar paintings, I could still spot it without a doubt. I was destined to be creative from the first moment I saw how a log cabin could be crafted from paper and sticks.

Grandpa's hustle

Where I'm from, you either hustle or you went hungry. It's pretty much that simple. My mother's father, Macie Thomas, taught me that. With just a sixth grade education, my grandfather fixed cars, built things, grew crops and occasionally gambled at the horse track. To say he was a jack-of-all-trades would be an understatement. Growing up, I never asked him for money. I had to ask him for work. My Grandpa didn't believe in handouts, work was all that man new. If wanted to go to the skating rink I called him to see if he had some work for me to do. If wanted to buy a game I asked him for work. He was tough, but the bond my grandpa and I had was stronger than most and I cherished every moment of it.

This stuff is not hard

First things first. This stuff is not hard, challenging, but not hard. Yeah, you're going to have to get better some technical stuff like video editing, copywriting, design, photography, strategy, etc., but it's not like going to law school or learning rocket science. Truth is, most creatives I know are self-taught. So as long as you put in the hours, you will become good at what you're creating. Once you're good at something, being great is only a matter of time and luck. We look at other creatives on TV or social media and think those people have super human creative powers. We think that they have more talent than us. We think they have the cheat code. This couldn't be further from the truth. In reality, if you ask them, they would probably tell you exactly what I'm telling you.

Delayed gratification

Lobster, as we know it today wasn't always a grand delicacy only the deepest of pockets could afford. Before the mid-19th century, lobster was considered poor man's food. It was so plentiful it was used as fertilizer. Lobster was held in such low esteem that it was given to prisoners in cans along with tuna. In the 16th and 17th centuries it was consumed mainly by European Royalty, and then in the 1950s the aristocrats of New York and Boston grew to like it and that's how it became popular. Today, lobster is going for at least twenty dollars a pound. Talk about delayed gratification. This was something I had to realize early on.

In 7th grade I entered a PTA Art contest and won first place for drawing a Tiger walking on water, and besides the people that gave me the award no one actually. In fact that same contest I won three years in a row. When I was begging musicians to let me shoot their music videos and design their album covers while I was in college, some of them treated it as joke. This is no shade to those people, but they just didn't see the vision and rightfully so. It wasn't up to them to see how dope I was, and what was up to me to show them.

Think of how many people that might treat your art like it's not worthy today or consider the job opportunities that passed you by. Nothing happens overnight. I went from begging people to let me design their logos for free to designing logos for some pretty great companies at prices I you wouldn't believe. That didn't happen overnight.

Success is not some microwaveable TV dinner. It's more like a slow cooked pot roast; the more you put in the better it is, but it will still take some time to get done. It's funny, because no one remembers waiting for weekends or after seven at night so you could take advantage of free minutes on your cell phone, or waiting for your internet to dial up. Technology, and life in general just moves fast, so people expect their success to move fast as well. Whether you believe in paying dues or not, doing so is still a major requirement for success. The quicker you come to this realization, the quicker you can obtain what you deem success is.

The monster in the room: anxiety

Before I graduated from high school, social media was only viewed on computers. You didn't have the weight of the social world at your fingertips. The only thing people cared about was who your top friends were on Myspace. Facebook was fairly new, so it really didn't hit us. Unfortunately, social media has plagued creatives. I am constantly surrounded by talented people who feel like they haven't done enough based on someone else's Instagram profile they are following. I know designers who are extremely good, but are super depressed because they're not getting the same press other designers are. I see musicians run their finances into the dirt trying to impress followers with expensive clothes and jewellery. This way of thinking has caused anxiety levels for creatives to go up, and creativity to go down amongst the community.

I was notorious for this way of thinking for years. All my classmates in college were going off getting jobs, posting pictures of travel, and creating dope memories. While I was trying to start a business and working a 9 to 5 design job. That sounded bad? In reality I was doing well. I had a job that I liked. My business was growing. I was too busy looking at other people's lives that didn't realize my life was dope as well. Stopped comparing my life to other people and started to run my own race. I started to live by my own terms.

Doesn't matter where you are from

I think we can all agree it truly doesn't matter where you're from. When I was young I use to think art was only for white middle-aged men who paraded around like imitations of Andy Warhol. Unfortunately, I didn't meet my first graphic designer that looked like me until I became one at the age of 20. Being the pretentious person I was, I quickly decided that if there were no designers where I was from, then I was going to be one. So from second grade on until the day I graduated from college, being a designer was on my mind. After leaving my hometown of Texarkana and moving to Houston for college, I quickly became involved in the art society of the big city. By staying persistent, eventually I was able to enter the advertising industry without having to go to New York and I gained clients in California,

Georgia, New York etc., all awhile living on the outskirts of Houston, Texas.

Austin Klenon, the famed writer of "Steal like an Artist" once wrote, "You don't have to live anywhere other than the place you are to start connecting with the world you want to be in." Fortunately, it didn't take reading his book for me to understand this. From day one I knew growing up in Texarkana, Texas didn't limit me. In fact, I always thought growing up there would give me the competitive edge when I did get the opportunity to explore the world. In this day and age we should have no complaints about being stifled by the elements of a small town. Even if you did want to throw a pity party about living in a small town, there are plenty of people who made it out of similar situations. So many that I don't care to name them. The internet has afforded us the opportunities of access and exposure, and you'd be a fool not to use it appropriately.

Take my late best friend Christopher Rockwell. When Chris decided that traditional college was way too much of a hassle, he moved back to our hometown and enrolled in Full Sail University online for mobile app development. When Chris graduated he secured a job working from home remotely for one of the nation's top Bible apps. Chris, like me, understood that it didn't matter where you were from, nor did it matter where you were physically. He was determined to be great no matter where he was. You can be in the hood, the suburbs, rural Texas, or Alaska; it just doesn't matter. Find ways to connect to online communities and show the world what you have to offer. Do whatever, but don't make where you live an excuse.

Takeaways:

- Being a creative entreprenuer is not hard, just takes work.
- It dont come overnight, have some patience.
- It doesn't matter where you are from or where you are at.
- Take advantage of the things around you.

Going from good to great

Chapter 2

"In its most simplistic form, branding is nothing but the art of consistency."

As a creative you don't get a cookie when you become good at your craft. Being good is just the bare necessity to survive in this world. Being great is whole different ball game. This level of achievement requires consistency, better network, great ideas, some luck, extreme discipline and finesse. How do we as creatives go from good to great? How can we go from amateur to the big leagues? How can our work go from in our basement to critical acclaimed? As subjective as those questions might be, we all want to be great at what we do, but that's easier said as done.

Wider perspectives, better work

In my life there were two times I got to experience what it was like to not be poor. Both of those times I lived with my uncle Tony in the suburbs of Houston. It was there living with him I interacted with my first people from Africa, Rich whites, and people of Middle Eastern decent. Prior to moving with my uncle all I had known was poor to middle class black and white people. At the time I didn't know this experience would shape me as a man yet alone a creative.

As a designer and marketer, I am often pulling ideas from my life experiences. This is what a lot of creatives do. When I look online or go through portfolios, I'm always curious about how artist come up with their pieces. I know every artist has a story or inspiration behind their work. So naturally, I'm interested in why. I believe once you get past the technical processes of creating, your perspective is the only thing that separates you from the next successful creative. With that being said, I also believe the only way to be more creative and to enhance your perspective is through experiences.

From your childhood through adulthood, your experiences shape the way you view the world. Experiences can come in different forms. When got my second job as graphic designer I was greeted with a potluck of ethnicities for co-workers. My boss was part Hispanic, our web designer was Nigerian, and our Tech guys were from Nepal, Jamaica and the Middle East. When I interacted with them I tried to understand their take on things and their culture. Overall, I've become more open and receptive to new experiences, and in the process my creative output grew more prosperous and productive. I've come to understand all creatives want the same thing, but not all creatives are raised the same and that's what shapes their perspective. Your perspective can be the reason you gain a client or a job, so don't brush it off like it doesn't mean anything.

Art of consistency

Jeff Bezos, the famed founder of Amazon stated, "Your brand is what people think of you when you're not in the room." In the beginning, your business brand is totally connected to your personal brand. Their coexistence is mandatory to your success.

In its most simplistic form, branding is nothing but the art of consistency. You mix that with your talent and you get powerful results. Early on I experienced art. With those experiences came abilities and with those abilities people started to take notice. This notoriety of me being an artistic person stuck with me through high school and college. Now I get paid to do art every day, people know me for my creative abilities, and my whole brand stands on the creative premise.

To say I knew what I was doing from second grade and on would be a lie. I didn't know I was branding myself back then, I was just a kid that loved drawing and painting. As I got older I began to realize what had occurred naturally, and began to be more intentional in my positioning. Tim Ferriss, the New York Times bestselling author of 4-hour Work Week, wrote that "Personal branding is about managing your name — even if you don't own a business — in a world of misinformation, disinformation, and semi-permanent Google records." Long before Tim wrote those words your reputation was still key to success; especially in my neighbourhood.

In my hometown your last name meant something to you, and you would do anything to protect it. The same principles stand with me to this day, but instead of protecting my name, I wanted to make one for myself. What better way to do that than to be consistent, and all consistency ever required was discipline. If art is what you want to do you should be doing it every day? You should be blogging about it every day. If people see you do and talk about art every day they will start to associate you with art. That's simple brand awareness.

USE THE INTERNET

1.Only share things you would like people to know about on social media.

I shared atleast one design a day for 3 months in order to get follwers to associate graphic design with me. I eventually dialed back the content when I started to get a lot of direct messages for work on Facebook that I didn't want to do.

2. Blog about your craft.

 I started blogging and even reached out to other blogs to feature me on their sites. When other people started talking about me people viewed me different.

3.Don't post frivolous content on your social media.

As entertainng as fight videos are and people pranking each other I dont post or repost them. The message that those videos portray dont align with my personal brand. If it was a design tutorial, then maybe i would share.

4.Show people the results of your work on social media.

About 80% of the content I posted was about art/graphic design, inspiration and business related. People will label you no matter what, atleast you can decide what label.

Be useful, personable, and practical

Ogilvy Advertising stated that "brands that want to matter have to be useful, practical and personable..." In this digital age it's not hard to find alternatives to the products and services we are selling. To ensure success, attention to details like the ones stated above are paramount.

How I became useful

There are many ways to be useful to people, so there's no wrong way. One of the ways I became useful was through design. Instead of creating art for myself I made it my mission to create art for others. My passion to become an artist evolved into my drive to become a designer. Contrary to popular belief there is a difference between a designer and artist, not just by definition, but also by objective. A designer creates with constraints and intentions, like designing movie poster or billboard. A designer might ask questions to understand what their clients' needs are. Whereas an artist creates with form and expression in mind. An artist won't ask for much input. Often an artist is not hired to create an effective magazine ad. Unfortunately we have some designers that think too much like artist and not enough artist thinking like designers.

How I became more personable

Face it, brands must be transparent. Whether you have a business or you're just doing freelance work you cannot be exempt from this rule. People want to know what you're doing as a creative. From my first Facebook post, I was transparent about my goals as a creative. Now I share stories, give advice, and show my creative process. These gestures allow people, who are all potential clients, to mentally invest themselves in what I stand for. People want to know the people they're giving their hard earned money to. If that means blogging about your day to day, writing a book, or speaking, either way you should be tapping into what makes you personable.

How I became more practical

I was a big fan of motivational speakers. I read many books and went to a lot of conferences that had motivational in the title. When I got serious about growing my business, I leaned toward more actionable and practical advice. The knowledge I was seeking was no longer inspirational; now it was tactical. I needed to know short cuts, contacts, and strategies to propel my company forward. In doing so I became more practical in the advice I was giving, my process was more efficient, and my clients' results increased. Clients will take practical any day, especially if it helps their bottom line. In the creative industry we sometimes can put a lot of fluff in our work. Your main objective should be producing results for clients.

Eliminate the fear of failure

Michael Jordan once said, "I can accept failing, everyone fails at something, but I can't accept not trying." Before investing $10,000 of my own money to plan and execute a festival I contemplated doing the festival for three years, because it was such a large investment and I felt I needed to learn more about throwing a festival. So, after three long years of researching, asking questions, and even attempting to intern for a huge festival in town, I decided to jumpstart the Space City Food Truck Festival. At the time, I didn't hear promoters meshing food trucks and a strictly hip hop artist into one big event. I thought that twist would add an advantage. I couldn't have my conscience eating at me for not pursuing my goals out of fear. If it's something you want to do, do it. Never let fear get in the way

Part of eliminating fear meant I had to isolate myself in order to rid myself of outside influences, like all the people I was surrounded by who dragged their feet. So surrounding myself with positive people or no people was crucial to me overcoming my fear of failure. I reminded myself where I had come from, which was the bottom of the barrel. And when you come from the bottom of the barrel, the only thing to do is rise to the top. I understood that I had nothing to lose and everything to gain. I also learned to set small goals that eventually aided one big goal. Instead of looking at a goal at a macro level I learned to minimize them into micro levels.

Example:

Your goal might be to start your own food truck business. That's a big task, but very doable. If you break this down into" let me get my LLC, then get a food stand." This makes your goals more attainable and eventually leads to you getting your food truck.

Fail fast

Consistency makes average people like me look like we know what we are doing. With that being said, I have consistently failed in just about everything I have done. I believe in failing fast, because when you fail fast, you learn fast. While everyone was thinking I was some renaissance man, I was collapsing more swiftly than they were which helped me learn more quickly than they were. I find it odd how people will put bits and pieces into a project over long periods of time and then quit. Often, the first thing they say is "Man, I should have quit earlier," or "If I knew then what I know now I would be better off." Although this feeling is inevitable, you can limit the sting if you fail fast. Trying new things quicker and taking more risk enables you to fail fast.

Throughout college, I tried new things and invested the little bit of money I had in anything that interested me. During my junior year of college I started a t-shirt company with a couple of friends called Ethnic Fleet Society, after that I tried managing a rap group called Hi-Def who had one local hit. Even though these ventures didn't work out as planned, I very quickly learned the cash intensive cost of manufacture clothing and also the stress that comes with managing a rap group who had a poor work ethic. As quick as I am saying these things, that's how quick I licked my wounds and was able to bounce back from those lessons. I never bit off more than I could chew, but I never wanted to regret not doing something I was interested either. Apart of failing fast is testing out things and realizing they might not be for you and moving on. Stop contemplating and start your business, start school, start that project you always wanted to do. If turns out to be what you expect move on.

Networking

Every so often I throw these black creative networking events called Marketing & Mimosas. The events combine the power of brunch and networking and spark dialogue about the challenges black creatives face. I feel these events are totally necessary due to the social awkwardness of networking while black. "Networking while black" is a thing none of us like to talk about, but is very much a real thing. It's when you are the only black person in the room and are forced to laugh at jokes that you clearly don't get. It's when people are afraid to talk to you, until one brave white guy walks up to you to spark a conversation. Now everyone is interested in hearing you philosophy. It's those times when I give you my card and follow up and never hear a word back from you. The list goes on. Apparently Marketing

& Mimosas was very necessary since it sold out on its first date. I realized my network had holes in it when I couldn't find any agency owners my age or ethnicity. Creating the event was part of the process of my fine tuning my network.

A part of fine tuning your network is to ask yourself why you are doing it. Is it to find a job, meet new creatives like yourself, get more gigs, or is it just to socialize? Being honest with yourself upfront allows you to manage your expectations and future frustrations with networking. The next thing you need to do is look at the network you already have and see if you are utilizing it right correctly. I once heard Sixty-three percent of people throw away business cards within the first week of getting them. If this is true then we are wasting a bunch of time taking and giving cards. For me personally, even in the digital age this practice is true. As many numbers as I put into my phone to possibly network with people, I have only actually used about ten percent of them. So I decided to compartmentalize the network I already had before adding more to my network.

I did this by separating my creative friends by their industry, profession, usage and sometimes their personality. Doing so allowed me to focus on what I needed in my network. In this method, expectations are clear within each circle you create, which leads to better efficiency when you collaborate. You're able to manage your network better and understand who is of most interest to you and who you can call on that has the expertise you need, etc. Once you have cleaned out your networking closet you can begin seeking new recruits into your creative fold. The next question is: Where do I find them?

Meet-ups and conferences have one thing in common; they are forced. Conferences boast heavy tickets and meet-ups are often a group of people who already know each other causing much more frustration to you and your networking needs. Truth is, networking should be organic and informative. Country clubs, fraternities, and professional organizations have mastered this. In fact, when I joined Kappa Alpha Psi, being a organic networking site was one of the reasons I stated for joining the organization, along with community service that it offered. The best networking takes place in personal and un-intrusive environments. So before you decide who you want to network with, understand why and where.

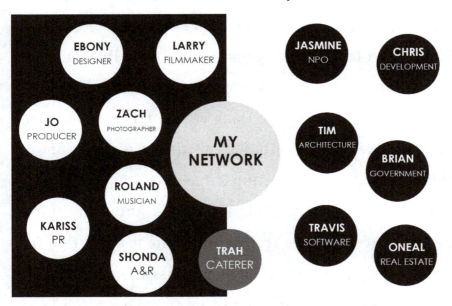

GOOD NETWORKING
- Ask yourself, why you are networking?
- Identify who you have in your network already and eliminate useless contacts.
- Identify where you will be networking.
- Focus on personal organic relations rather than forced professional relationships.

Communicate well

One of the biggest tools you will have as a creative entrepreneur is your mouth. No matter how fancy your pitch deck or RFP response is, your oratory skills will often be the deciding factor when it comes to landing a gig or contract. During my undergraduate years at Prairie View A&M University I took a Business Communication class with Dr. Reginald Bell. The class forever changed my life. Prior to that class I had never gave a presentation without saying "um" or "huh" or using flash cards. His class tasked us with learning a subject, writing a speech about the subject, and presenting a speech. Completing his class gave me the confidence to talk about anything in front of anyone. Great communication skills are one of the pillars of being a successful entrepreneur. Now, whenever I walk in a room to give a pitch I get excited because I know I am equipped with the right oratory skills.

COMMUNICATION IS **KEY**

 Know what the hell you're talking about. There's nothing worse than looking smart but sounding dumb. Know what you're selling, what your processes are, and the results you rendered for other clients.

 Make eye contact. The lack of eye contact shows your insecurities, and no one wants to give their money to someone who lacks the confidence to do their job.

 Pace yourself. Don't try to fast talk. Engage with them on their tone and level volume. When you talk fast you tend to repeat yourself and say unnecessary things. Also, people might think you're trying to con them.

 Move around. If you are presenting to people, move around them and engage with certain people on each side of the room.

RESOURCES

PROFESSIONAL NATIONAL ORAGNIZATIONS YOU SHOULD CHECK OUT FOR NETWORKING OPPORTUNITIES.

American Marketing Association

American Institute for Graphic Arts

AdColor

Marcus Graham Project

American Advertising Federation

National Association of Black Journalist

The One Club

Black Girls Code

Small Business Development Center

Colorcomm

National MBA Association

Organization of Black Designers

Value proposition and
positioning

CHAPTER 3

What is value proposition? What does it mean to you as an individual and a company? How can we enhance it? At its core a value proposition is the reason people should do business with you. What are the benefits of purchasing your creative services versus the other guy? An entrepreneur should be able to answer these questions before he or she even start their business. Unfortunately, as individuals we don't think about what really makes us unique as person, so how can we even imagine what makes our business unique. When I was designing t-shirts in college my main goal was to show people why they should buy from us instead of the other twenty brands on campus at the time. In retrospect, we all sold the same product and none of us ever had more clout than the other. Our biggest accomplishment was selling a shirt to a kid in Hawaii. None of the clothing brands on campus had a unique value proposition even though all of us claimed we were different from the rest. I'll be the first to admit we were not. Besides our designs, nothing really set us apart.

That all changed when I stumbled across a brand named Sevenly on a T-shirt business blog. Sevenly was different; it had a unique value proposition. The t-shirt added a social component to its business model. Each week the company chose a different charity and designed a shirt inspired the charity's mission. For every shirt the brand sold, Sevenly donated seven bucks to the charity that had inspired the shirt design. Their strategy proved itself and now the company is a global brand and has donated over five million dollars to tons of charities. Even though I stopped selling shirts, I took that strategy of creating a value proposition and have applied it to every business I've ever created since then.

As creative entrepreneur you have to understand that it's not enough to just design, or play an instrument. You have to find your value proposition and give people a reason to do business with you.

Value proposition as an individual

Discovering and understanding your value proposition as an individual creative is paramount to getting your foot in the door of the industry you desire. Your value proposition is simple; it's what you are good at. It is that one thing no one can take from you. What is that one thing that you can do in your sleep? Unlike a business, your individual value proposition isn't wrapped around the idea of uniqueness; it is wrapped around the idea of utility and purpose. When you step into a room full of people you should be able to walk in with your head up high because you know what you can offer. The leverage I created as a designer and filmmaker helped me navigate the industry as an individual creative. The one thing I was really good at allowed me to meet powerful people and establish relationships. At this point, being the jack of all trades is overrated and useless. Narrow down your expertise and let the chips fall where they may.

Positioning

Again, I like to think I was somewhat ahead of the curve when it came to positioning myself as an individual creative. Even before I knew what vision and mission statements were, I created a blueprint for my personal brand to go by. Basically, positioning is when a company or individual has a creed or promise to follow. Retail giant Target's positioning statement is, "Style on a Budget "; their statement is the driving force behind their product, marketing, and operational decisions.

Me being the entrepreneur I was in college, I decided to create a statement to help guide my design career. It was, "Never Sacrifice Quality for Quantity" and it was the best decision I could ever have made at that time. I took this positioning and wrote in on my walls and in my notebooks. I took this attitude on all my projects. No matter the size of the budget, I always gave it my best work. No matter how much I needed the money, I never took on more projects that I couldn't do my best work at. I became a stickler for details and processes because I knew they would enhance the quality of my work. When I got jobs as a designer I would fight for anything that helped increased my quality of work, like better equipment and more training. That positioning I made when I was on my way out of college helped guide all my decisions, and it is why I have been successful so far.

Positioning also allowed me to gain the clients that i desired. Looking at large agencies like Oglivy & Mather and Droga 5 I dreamed of the type of clients they had. I wanted to get clients that would pay premium prices for my work. I wanted to get clients that would get me more clients. In order to get those clients positioning was my only option.

Get the Clients you want

There is a process to getting the clients that you want. In a perfect world you would land a contract with Nike straight of college and be known across the globe for your abilities to forecast design trends. But, since this world is not a utopia, you and I both have to rely on our God given talents and some strategy to get us the clients we want.

Decide early what type of client you want

When I first started designing for money my clients were party promoters looking to get flyers designed and local rappers wanting mixtape covers. I always wanted to do more than to design flyers for 40 bucks. I wanted to get paid good to design for businesses and corporations. So my junior in college I started to position myself around decision makers. While I was in school I talked to all my professors who I knew had businesses. I attended local chamber of commerce meetings early on, where all the business owners resided even before I had an official business. Before I graduated I wanted make sure everyone knew me for design and I knew what type of clients I wanted.

You might need to fake till you make it

When I first started Kreadiv & Koo it was just me. I had 2 clients, no employees, no structure and no way real way of getting new business. I was intrigued by every ad agency on Madison Avenue and I wanted to design brand identities like them. Agencies like Pentagram were creating timeless logos for prestige companies, logos that I knew I could design just like them. But before I would be able to get those prestige clients I had to figure out a way to demonstrate that I had the premium capabilities that Pentagram had. At the time I only had a restaurant and horse training facility as my clients. I put together a decent website and added my friends as employees on the site. After asking many businesses to let me design pro bono I finally got a few to contact me back. I learned as much as I could about every position that an agency had. I figured if I was going to act like I was running a full-service agency I needed to know how every position an agency worked. When you have no experience and no connections, it's hard for people to take a chance on you. It is a dilemma that has always plagued the creative community. Sometimes you got to do what you got to do. As time went on, my clients grew larger and budgets got bigger. The companies I wanted to do business with eventually reached out to me instead of the other way around. In its basest form, positioning is calculated decisions that help you obtain what you desire. In the end I got those prestige clients that I wanted and won some awards along the way.

Build real relationships with real people

90% of my clients I have stem from a relationship, not some networking event. When I was college I made it my mission to talk to professors who I knew had businesses. I picked their brain anytime I could. I hung around people that were dreamers and were determined. If you were a creative I wanted to build with you and it was that simple. I gained some friendships and business in the process.

Out of sight, out of mind

Once you understand your position, you need to let people know what you do. For some reason, talented and creative people feel the talent they have is enough. They think people will notice them just off of sheer talent. Most people who think like that end up being broke, starving artists trying to relive the life of the broke artist who became rich in their afterlife. Let's face it, if you want to make money as a creative, you got to be able to sell yourself, and one of the first ways to do that is to make sure your work is visible.

Lucky for us, we are in the age of information were everything is social and meant to be shared. Social media platforms like Facebook and Instagram are made by creatives and meant for creatives like us. Your work should definitely be shown on Facebook and Instagram. I personally always made sure I had a business page even though I was doing freelance; I had every intention to make my side-hustle a business. Social media is not enough for exposure. Yeah, you might get a few likes and several broke rappers asking for ten dollar mixtape covers, but these are not the people you want to pursue. The ways you get exposure should be diverse if you want a diverse client base that pays. Some of your potential clients might be at award shows, some of them might be at conferences, some of them might surf Behance or Fiverr.com. You need to do your research and find out where your potential clients might be. This is not a one size fit all situation.

Shaping your expertise

David C. Baker wrote, "We struggle with making good positioning decisions for ourselves because as risk-taking entrepreneurs we can hardly bring ourselves to say no." The author of "The Business of Expertise" was explaining the mistakes creatives make when it comes to positioning themselves through client work and other projects. I myself have been a victim of this mentality for most of my career. I thought every problem a client came to me with was worth solving or every project was the right project to challenge me. In a nutshell, I was either too scared, too broke, or too stubborn to say no to projects that didn't fully serve the progression of me or my company. Although your value proposition is not defined as your ability to say no, it is a key driver in your ultimate position. If you want to be a corporate dj, eventually you will have to stop taking those club gigs. When I decided that my agency would only focus on the education sector I had to stop pitching other types of business. This is easier said than done when you're broke and upcoming, but their will come time were you will have to choose a narrower path to get the clients that you want.

Tip: If you have to do work that's not in your niche don't put it on your site or publicize it.

You're an expert; not an narcissist

In the midst of this positioning and value proposition talk, being expert at what you do should be every creative's goal, but that quest for authoritative knowledge can sometimes cloud your mind. Google what an expert is and you'll find, "An expert is a person who has a comprehensive and authoritative knowledge of or skill in a particular area." As creatives, we like to see ourselves as experts. In some cases we are. Some of us take the word expert too far. I mean, look at the definition of "authoritative knowledge." Really? Sounds like something a control freak would say. The truth is, being creative expert is so subjective in most cases that nobody has any authority to judge whether something is the right or wrong method to use. I understand doctors being experts and engineers being experts. Those are the people you want to have full authoritative knowledge over a subject, especially when your life is on the line. I'm not saying our creative jobs are not just as important. We have to lighten up on this situation of being an expert. Honestly flaunting your expertise should only matter when you're trying to pitch an idea or win a new client, otherwise it can seem just plain narcissism.

I think we all can sometimes be so stuck on ourselves and disregard other creative's perspectives. Sometimes we've got to wake up and realize we are students forever, and we should never turn down the chance to learn new things. The best experts never stop learning. Often times we think the titles we possess give us the power. In reality your talent is what gives you power, not your job title.

A	B	C	D
Look at your competitors, and find out what they are doing.	Figure out what's missing in the industry.	Create your value proposition around what's missing in the industry.	Communicate your value proposition to potential clients through website, networking, etc.

What does your client's profile look like?

Age	
Gender	
Income	
Industry	
Location	
Purchase Habits	
Education	

TOP POTENTIAL CLIENTS

1._____

2._____

3._____

Carpool your dreams

Chapter 4

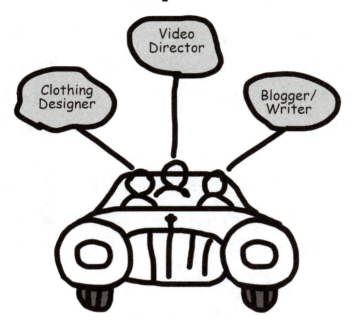

Once, while I was speaking in Washington D.C. on brand storytelling I overheard a conversation about how horrible D.C. traffic was and how the cost of living in the city was one of the main causes of the constant traffic jams . One of the conference attendees had stated that most people that work in the city have to commute out of the area because they can't afford to stay there. About mid-way into the conversation I started to hear these ladies mention the word slugging. Of course, I was intrigued, because

I wanted to know what a middle-aged white lady meant by slugging. Turns out, slugging is a form of transportation in the area. In a nutshell, people carpool to work with strangers they pick up from pre-determined locations. Car-poolers stand in line at each spot and wait for the next driver. It sounds like Uber, but this was all free. It dawned on me that if we can carpool together for free to work with strangers, than why can't we carpool together for free to our dreams?

I never understood how two or more people could be headed to the same place at the same time and get into different cars. The price of gas is way too high for that nonsense. I feel that same way with dreams. I started to look at the cost of following your dreams, the price to relocate, education, networking, and equipment, I wondered why people don't carpool their dreams. Have you ever found three people who wanted to break into the same industry? They're all working against one another or at least not working together, and they don't understand they're spending much more energy trying to accomplish their goals on their own than they would with the help of others. Granted, sometimes you have no choice but to do the work by yourself, but if you don't have to work in silos, don't do it.

Just like slugging, the next thing I had to do was to locate car-poolers. That was through networking, through a schooling/college, or in other areas you can find people who are serious about their craft. When I was in college there were few of us trying to start businesses, so sought out the ones that did. I wanted to surround myself with self-starters and people that were hungry for success just as much as I was. I searched for people that didn't want to wait on a college degree to do what they wanted. I didn't want to have to drag people to meetings, or beg people to show up to events.

Once I was able to surround myself with a group of passionate creatives I quickly begin to notice my strength and weakness. This self-discover allowed me to rely on people that were better at certain things than I was and also created opportunities for me to step up in be a leader. When I first started my company I had eight individuals whom I believed wanted the same thing I wanted. I couldn't pay them one cent, but they were interested in building the company and achieving their goals, just like me. We all had full-time jobs and eventually wanted to leave them. As grand as it sounds to make it on your own, no one does. We all have people that help us get where we want to go. Start collaborating now.

When you embark on this journey of creative entrepreneurship you must understand that everyone you deal with outside of your creative team are collaborators as well. These people are your friends and family. They might not be helping you decide what color a fabric should be or creating a strategy for a campaign. They are helping decide what schools your kids go to or creating a personal finance plan for the future for you. With that being said the way you handle your relationships with your friends and family are vital.

Friends

Every uncharted path has detours and roadblocks that add time to the journey. Our lives as creatives are no different from the roads we travel on. Like pot holes and constructions signs, we might have friends and family hindering or blocking our way to success. Unfortunately, the people we love so dearly sometimes can cause detours and road blocks in our life. As a creative, it is extremely important that you choose wisely the people you allow in your life. People who hang around that have no vision will cause you to lose sight of yours. Sometimes we mistake acquaintances for friends. This can cause us to hold onto relationships we should let go of. It just doesn't make sense to be friends with people that don't add value to your life. As an undergrad I met a lot of acquaintance that I mistook as my friends. You have to know the difference. A friend is a loyal supporter of your work. Friends will be honest with you even if you don't like it; in fact, they might only agree with you fifty percent of the time. An acquaintance will only you give bits and pieces of the truth. These are the road blocks on our creative journey. It is extremely careless to think its fine to waste your energy on people who are neutral towards you gaining success. You should only be giving energy to people that give you energy. If you have to think someone has your best interest than their not your friend, you should know.

Family

Under the pressures of survivor's remorse, I felt a need to help my family that was back home. Pretty much any successful person can attest to the inevitably feeling sorry for your less fortunate loved ones. Truth is, there is a doorway to success and only one person at a time can fit through. You can't squeeze two people in at a time, only one. Family is important, but right now you are more important. As harsh as it seems, we can't let family distract us from the task at hand. Enjoy the time you spend with them, but don't let the pressures of wanting to help them hinder you from helping yourself. These are the detours that will come often; you just have to be strong enough to avoid them or limit them.

Pick and choose your battles and let your family know what you are trying to accomplish. Hopefully they understand, but if they don't try not to lose any sleep over it.

Entrepreneurship DNA

Joe Abraham coined the concept of the BOSI chart which breaks down the four types of entrepreneurs. During my senior year at college I stumbled upon a video of him teaching the concept to a group of inspiring entrepreneurs. There are the builders, people who loved to create things from the ground up; they use strategy a lot. There's the opportunist, people who want to make a quick buck and are willing to risk more than the average entrepreneur. Next you have the specialist, the person who sticks to what he or she knows; typically making their money in one industry. Finally, you have your innovators, they only want to create; they don't care about the business. It totally made sense. If I knew my strong points, I could find someone to compensate were I was weak at. In my case, I was born a builder; however, as creative as I wish I had better ideas.

So I reached out to innovators to join my carpool. People that had a different views than me and fresh ideas. This approach came in handy when I started my festival. I knew I could rally people to join my team, and understood I would be that glue to hold things together. I needed more specialist on my team, so I tapped my college buddies Karriss who did PR and Shonda who was in the music business. Their specialities not only allowed me to do what I did best, but really pushed the festival's popularity forward. The BOSI chart allowed me to be a better leader and creative.

Partners

A business partner is the second most important relationship you will ever have, next to your spouse. In some cases, you will spend a lot of time with them, debating with them and trusting them. So it's important that, like any relationship, you take your time with making it official.

During college I attempted to start my company with business partners, but that didn't work out. Even as I write this book I am in a vesting period with a potential business partner who I have sub-contracted work to for the last couple of months. Technically, a vesting period is the period of time before shares in an employee stock option plan or the benefits in a retirement plan are unconditionally owned by an employee. But for me, I'm using the word to define this time when I'm trying to see if this guy and I can collaborate together, and if he can hold his own in unique situations. I need to fully trust him and his thought leadership before I can give him a piece of the pie. Finding a partner is not that complicated, it just takes time. If you're not having any luck finding a partner, don't get discouraged; having one might not be for you. If you are looking for a partner early on here are some tips to help you.

Lets Talk Partners

1. Don't be desperate to find a partner.

2. Remember your Entrepreneur DNA; focus on partners that help your weaknesses.

3. Collaborate on small projects before you sign anything.

4. Go through a vesting period before you give them any ownership of your company.

5. Make sure they have some skin in the game and have already invested in their craft.

6. Check their egos; they need to be able to be criticized as well as hand out criticism.

7. Check their work ethics; if they party every weekend, they may be slackers. Are they procrastinators? Are they self-starters?

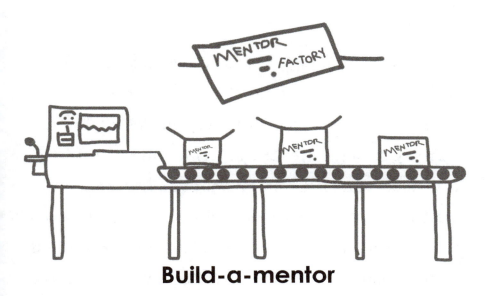

Build-a-mentor

Let's face it. Finding a mentor is harder than finding a job. People in that industry might be too busy, too bossy, or too damn whack to help you or bring you under their wing. Mentorship isn't something you can sweep underneath the rug. Even more important is that you find the right mentor. Luckily for me, I always had my Uncle Tony. My Uncle Tony was a successful car salesman who eventually became a dealership owner. Although he made a big impact in life for the most part, my uncle then didn't teach me anything about my profession. In fact, I might have taught him a few things about brand positioning and marketing. The only thing I did learn from my uncle was that I could come from nothing and make something. By watching him excel from small town

Texarkana to running a million dollar business it gave me hope. In the beginning, that was all I needed. This pattern of taking from different professionals has been my strong suit while searching for mentorship. The fact that not one person has intentionally tried to mentor me is quite disturbing, and is the sole reason I actively try to mentor young and old professionals that want to enter in the creative industry or entrepreneurship. So, in attempting to find guidance, I created a Frankenstein mentor, a combination of people I both knew and didn't know. As creepy as it sounds, this method has helped guide my decisions like a mentor should.

Like I said, my uncle was my first mentor, and he helped spark my interest in business. I saw that he was a fearless investor and was always willing to bet on himself. These were the qualities I instilled into my business acumen. Then there was my marketing professor Dr. Rick Baldwin, who throughout my career has supported any new idea I had as he has done for many other students of his. His thirst for innovation and support for youth is something I hope to match one day. Next was my first boss, Bridgett Ross, a very sweet lady who gave me my first shot as a designer and consultant. The year I spent with her I watched her keep her composure like no other person could under rough situations. In addition to her ability to stay calm in the midst of chaos, her people skills were even better. I vowed to treat my clients the way she did hers. Besides the group of people I actually had physical encounters with I also drew people like Audrey Gilbreath, Aaron Draplin, Lewis Williams, and many other creatives I admired and studied from afar. In retrospect, I realized none of those people had mentored me full-on like I wanted them to. I understood it was up to me to soak in any information that was available or whenever I was around them. Overall, I have come to the conclusion that mentorships don't have to be either physical or intentional. The main reason why most people desire mentorships is access to knowledge and opportunity. I can confidently say I had access to knowledge and I soaked it up like a sponge even if the mentor wasn't physically near me, or intentionally trying to teach me. The opportunity part, I had to make myself.

Gaining Access

Direct messaging an executive

Is it possible to build meaningful relationships over social media with all the fake news, catfishing, and lack of morality the internet brings? I believe it is very much possible, but not just on any platform. The New York Post wrote, "If you wouldn't ask someone for a job an hour after meeting them at a networking event, you shouldn't pitch a perfect stranger via a LinkedIn message." While this is true, the instant gratification social media brings can deprive us from building solid networks via the internet. People want complete interaction the minute they follow you, or else they unfollow. The subtle approach to social networking is completely dying. When I was searching for answers as to why I felt locked out of the advertising industry, I couldn't find anyone to provide answers in person. The only option I had was to reach out to executives on LinkedIn. I had tried this before, but most of the messages were ignored. For the most part I would send a general message to high profile LinkedIn users hoping that they would bite. I took a different approach this time, unlike my last attempts, I decided to research the people I wanted advice from. I watched their interviews and read articles about them. When reached out to them via direct message I started off the by telling them how much they inspired me (they really did) and next, I mentioned articles I'd read in relation to them or interviews I saw them in. To me, this showed them I wasn't just some random kid looking for a handout. I was on a mission and I wanted them to help me. My intentions where clear, and so were my expectations. With that approach I was able to talk to advertising agency owners, chief creative officers, and directors. Overall, this approach to social networking was effective, and afforded me a lot of information that I wouldn't have been privy to had I taken the same lazy approach I normal took.

Nicolas Cole, founder of Digitalpress.com, explained what mentors look for in a mentee by saying, "Someone who isn't afraid to say, 'I don't know what I don't know.' Someone who not only opens themselves up to being taught, but is also extraordinarily appreciative." In order to gain access to powerful and smart people you have to undress your ego and let them know you want to learn. This lets them know you are willing to be taught and, more importantly, you are less likely to waste their time. Through e-mail, I approached American Advertising Federation hall of famer Audrey Gilbreath and Burrell Communications Chief Creative Officer Lewis Williams. I didn't think they would respond, but they did. Don't quite remember what I said to Lewis, but I'm almost certain it went something like this.

"Hey Lewis, you don't know me from a can of paint, but I wanted to reach out to you for advice. First of all thank you for inspiring me. I recently got a chance to view your interview on Conversations with Giants and it was great. I have been aspiring to become a creative director for the last five years. I want to know what it takes to build a good portfolio without the experience of a top agency or attending a fancy portfolio school. I graduated from HBCU and started a design and marketing company after I couldn't find a job in the industry. Although I've had minor success, I still feel shut out from the industry. At this point I truly don't know what to do. If you could guide me with some practical advice I would be extremely grateful."

It worked. He scheduled a call with me and we talked for an hour. I approached Audrey the same way and she invited me to visit her office where she reviewed my resume and gave me some really good advice on creative direction. I wouldn't have gotten access to that knowledge had I not humbled myself and expressed my willingness to learn.

Curate Knowledge

Once you've gained access into the movers and shakers, information will come at you at a hundred miles per hour. You'll be the fly on the wall listening to all the juicy details, but none of the information means anything if you can't interpret whether you need it or not. In the midst of learning from these involuntary mentors you will come across a lot of advice that is either bad or frivolous to your agenda. This is where the curation of knowledge should take place. When I was building my mentor I only took things seriously that benefited me directly. I didn't need inspiration, I needed practicality. You have to decide what you need from them and specifically extract that. As methodical as it sounds, it's important to only take what you will use.

Like my home girl Jessey. For the sake of not being sued I'll call her Jessey. She was fresh out of college when she landed a job as copywriter. She had no mentors at the time and was seeking refuge in any person that would lend her their time. Very smart and ambitious, she sought out mentorship from her boss. Her boss was just that, a boss. Someone who only ordered people around and didn't really get her hands dirty when the team was down. When she got a new job at our company I quickly realized that the qualities of her previous boss had leaked into her leadership style as well. Needless to say she quickly realized our office was ran a little bit differently. Before I left that job, I had a heart-to-heart with her and explained that she didn't need to take everything from her past boss; only the things she felt were necessary for her progression. Sometimes we do take bad habits from good people, but it's up to us to separate the good from the bad.

I am not saying real mentorships can't be obtained or shouldn't be sought after. If you're one of the lucky ones you will find a mentor that helps and provides you with opportunities. In the event you don't find that mentor, just look around there's a piece of mentor in all of us.

Dear young people

During my childhood I lived on this dead-end road, and on this road lived mostly senior citizens. Along with my grandparents and great-grandparents were Mr. Brown, Cousin Leon, Mr. Farris, the Benton's and several other people who were old also. These people were my first customers in just about every venture I had as a child. When I sold candy, I went to Mr. Brown first. When I was collecting aluminium cans, I went to my grandmothers. When I was doing yard work I went to Cousin Leon. I learned to respect older people and, more importantly, I learned how to gain their trust. Fast-forward twenty years and eighty percent of my clients are older than me by twenty or more years. I can't help but think my upbringing with older people had something to do with that.

Dealing with clients of older generations can be very beneficial. They have the money, they are in some cases more established, and they have a wealth of knowledge. Clients like these are what you want and need to grow. Don't get me wrong its always a plus when you can do business with young clients who might understand you better, but don't shy away from more seasoned clients. Sure, the conversation might be different and more challenging, but you will find in most cases the challenge is very rewarding.

Veteran Creatives

There is also a misconception amongst millennials that generation x and baby boomers don't want to listen. We often think, they think we are entitled snowflakes. When in reality, we are great listeners and love to hear from our OG's. I myself have always been attracted to the wisdom older people bring. The problem sometimes is that older people have issues connecting with us. We don't want to be told to get off our ass when we are working just as hard as the past generations have. We are not looking for hand-outs. We are looking for opportunities. Most people in my generation are willing to work day and night for the passion we love. Connecting with a younger generation of creatives shouldn't be about pointing out our flaws; it should be about pointing us in the right direction. I believe this is the right way to connect. If you don't come correct with us, you will have a hard time connecting with us. In hindsight, veteran creatives can be more results oriented and reserved. They want to know if you can get the job done no matter what. No excuses. That is something I always admired about the vets, their no nonsense ideology.

We have to understand that the veteran creative love what they do just like we love what we do. This way of thinking has to be vice versa. Veteran creatives have to be willing to receive advice and collaborate with us new creatives, and teach us their tricks.

> **YOU** CANT DO IT **ALONE.** **CARPOOL** YOUR **DREAMS.**

Some of the biggest financial and creative successes have been the results of my collaborating with creatives of all generations. We shut ourselves off and create unwarranted disadvantages if we don't collaborate with each other. Younger creatives miss out on the wisdom. Veteran creatives miss out on opportunities to continue to grow.

Might have to do it alone

Carpooling your dreams can take time, effort and you slowly choosing the right people to collaborate with. In the meantime, you might have to rely on yourself. The best creatives usually have no problems with this. We flourish in silos, but don't mind the activity of collaboration. To get things done right, you might just have to do it yourself. This might cause you to wear many hats, but so be it. Otherwise, you will be continually seeking help when you don't need it or constantly falling in the lanes of inconsistent people. When I first embarked in film I shot all my projects alone. I was a one-man crew riding through the streets of Houston shooting any and every one. By doing it this way I got my mistakes in without the negative feedback of collaborators, and also was able to form my own point of view on filming without the influence of a collaborator. Although at some points I wished I did have help, I felt it was the best way for me to start. I believe your creative career is like a Broadway play, some people will get off and some people will get ON, but the show must still go on.

WHAT'S YOUR ENTREPRENEURSHIP DNA

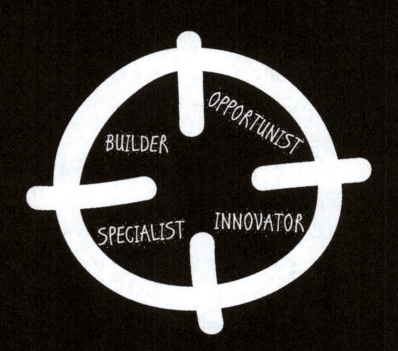

BUILDER

OPPORTUNIST

SPECIALIST

INNOVATOR

THANKS JOE ABRAHAM-BOSI FRAMEWORK

5

Handle your business

Chapter 5

Handle Your Business

> **As a creative, your goal is to make whatever idea you have, better.**

Too often I come across creatives who just don't do good business. They are horrible in communicating with their clients, going after new business, or they just don't understand customer service. The formalities that come with conducting business seem to blow past them; mostly because they are too lazy to conduct business correctly, or they simply don't understand how to navigate entrepreneurship. I myself have never had this problem because I fell in love with business the same time I fell in love with art. While I was drawing cartoons in second grade, I was also selling candy on the side. Being a creative entrepreneur is a difficult task and sometimes you will have to put business before being a creative. Sometimes you will have to limit the time on a project because its costing money by the hour, or you may have to participate in brainstorming meetings when you'd rather be creating. The truth is, the decision to put business before art is only bad when you sacrifice quality in your work to do so. Make no mistake, I will never tell a creative to sacrifice quality just to save a few bucks. The fact is, creatives shouldn't shy away from doing business, in fact, and they should welcome it. When you add the mind-set of a business person to the innate creative in you, the possibilities are limitless. You develop a respect for (ROI) Return on Investment and design theory. You manage budgets and you creatively direct. Being a creative entrepreneur means doing this and much more, and if you get to it quickly, by the time you have fully developed your skill set, handling your business will be second nature.

Start the business first

I think creatives should start the business first, even if they're not good enough to make money at first. It may not sound right, but trust me on this one. When I was in college designing flyers for my peers for pennies on the dollar, I still had a DBA (Doing Business As) and a business bank account. At the time I might have been jumping the gun, but by the time I started making real money I had experience in balancing my books, enhancing SEO on my site, and writing contracts. In the beginning, none of my business skills weren't as polished as they are now, but running my small business in college allowed me to make business mistakes early on without the high cost of penalties of running a business as adult with a family.

Besides learning about mistakes, having a business back then allowed my business to create a credit history which came in handy later on down the line when I was looking for funding to expand. Imagine your dad giving you an established business when you finished college. Unfortunately we don't all have that opportunity. So I created that myself. This was my way of creating a safety net. I even used my business as an internship and got college credit for it. In retrospect, starting my business first before I became the award-winning creative director I am today, enabled me to become who I am today, if that makes any sense.

Somethings you will need to start a business

1. Get a DBA or LLC
2. Get a free EIN
3. Open up a bank account
4. Build a professional site
5. Get business licenses

Nothing is new under the sun

There is a difference between a designer and an artist. Artists use perspective as their inspiration, designers use constraints. In business we are designers. We take the challenges of our clients and design around that, hoping we can solve their problem. Before I designed, I painted. My love for the arts eventually evolved into my thirst for originality. Everyone around me was trying to be original and super different. I was obsessed with creating things no one had done before. This drove me to spend months on pieces. As an artist, this way of thinking might not be a problem, but as a business man, you won't be able to get anything done. Even though human beings are very different from each other, it is a rarity if we create things that no one else has thought of or created before. Pure originality is almost a thing of the past. Truth is, I don't think the world needs another original idea. We just need to make the ones we've have, better. As a creative, your goal is to make whatever idea you have, better. You will tire yourself trying to be the "Original Gangsta" of every idea. When I started my food truck festival I knew there were a tons of events like it, that fact didn't discourage me. I added live hip hop music, hookah, and beer pong; those things made it different from the other food truck festivals in town. Explore new ideas to solve old problems. Redesign, recycle and recreate art. Remould ancient structures from your perspective. Just remember nothing is new under the sun.

Throw a party for your clients

If you're conducting business, creditability is extremely important, especially among your peers and potential clients. Sometimes social media, networking, and awards are not enough credit to get you new business. Sometimes you're just going to have to throw a party for your potential client. As I mentioned, when I first started my agency one of things I did was host events like my Marketing & Mimosas. I rented a space, called a friend of mine who was a caterer and linked up with an organization with the same demographics to help fund it. I wrote all the expenses off on my taxes as marketing dollars. After the event I sent out a press release to people who wrote about black creatives and managed to get on a couple of blogs to write about my company. It was a great networking event for everyone with good food, but my main goal was to showcase my company's talents to people in the industry who, from my perspective, were all potential clients. Most of the time those events led to more traffic on my sites, increased my followers on social media and gave us at least two inquiries. This method has been used by non-profits for years. They sponsor charity event galas and invite potential donors, hoping they donate. You and your company should be no different.

How I Built My Creditability

•Curated events that invited industry potential clients

•Won awards, followed by press releases to potential clients

•Blogged about my process

•Wrote this book

•Networked with industry influencers.

How much?

In the beginning, you will be doing things for free. The question is, how long should you be doing things for free? In my opinion, after your work has reached a standard level of quality and you have gained the confidence to repeat those results you should begin charging. People should know you can do the work and you should have a good reputation early on. One of the pricing tactics I started doing was setting a minimum price for myself as a freelancer, I called it my standard creative rate. I wouldn't do anything lower than $125. Sometimes that was an hourly rate and sometimes that fee was a flat project rate for a flyer. If a person couldn't pay that, they couldn't get my services at all.

You have to be confident and consistent to not fall into your own hole of cheap labor. I was tempted to create a flyer for $50 or a logo for $100, I stayed strong; stuck to my creative standard rate which was $125. It's the only way people will see your work as being premium and having true value. If we don't value our time or work, how can we expect our clients to value our time and work?

Before I graduated from college I created a chart similar to the one below that not only gave me goals to obtain, but it also set a standard to aim for. Your chart might be different from mine, but it is imperative that you set goals and standards of your own to inspire to.

SKILL LEVEL	YEARS OF EXPERIENCE	TYPE OF CLIENTS	PRICE RANGE	PROJECT EXAMPLE
NOVICE	1-2 YEARS	FRIENDS FAMILY PEERS	$0-$300	A FRIENDS START UP LOGO
AMATEUR	3-5 YEARS	LOCAL BUSINESS & INDIVIDUALS	$300 -$5,000	LOCAL RAPPER'S MUSIC VIDEO
PRO-AMATEUR	5-7 YEARS	MID-SIZED COMPANIES	$5,000- $10,000	ART DIRECTION FOR A LOCAL MAGAZINE
ELITE	7+ YEARS	MID TO LARGE COMAPNIES	$10,000+	REGIONAL MARKETING CAMPAIGN

Sales Funnel

As a creative entrepreneur you're going to be constantly selling. In order to be cash positive, this process needs to be constantly tweaked and perfected. Before I created my sales funnel, most of the time I was winging it. I would just walk into a restaurant and ask if they needed any graphic design, and sometimes that actually worked. But in order to land clients on a consistent basis, when I approached them or even when they approached me, I realized I needed to have a sales funnel. Now, the proper definition of a sales funnel is the buying process that companies lead customers through when purchasing products, in other words, how to get people to buy your stuff; in our case, creative services. In reality, it's a simple process and something you have probably been doing your whole life.

1. Let people know what you do and what your company has to offer, whether it's via social media, e-mail, or just plain word-of-mouth. You need to make sure people are aware you exist.

2. Make sure the work you display on your site or social media is good and is the type of work you want more of. People will be googling you, make sure they see what you want them to see.

3. When a potential client calls or e-mails, listen to their needs and wants first. Then follow up with budget questions to find out if they are in your price range before you commit to the project. Also, this gives you the opportunity to demonstrate why you're worth the premium price.

4. After negotiating price and scope of work, send them a short contract showing the scope of work, how long the project would take, the cost of the project and few other company policies.

5. Next, send fifty percent deposit invoices. Sometimes companies only do Net 30, in which the client has thirty days after the project is done to pay you. Some companies can receive PayPal or stripe invoices and some can only send you a check. Be prepared to accept either.

6. In some cases, midway through the project, ask for another twenty-five percent of the budget if that was stated in the contract.

7.After they approve the project, get the rest of your money and send them the deliverables in a zip file or link. If you send project files in a link, make sure to let them know that the link expires in a certain amount of time.

8. Ask for referrals, suggestions, and testimonies as you do a final follow up.

Depending on your type and maturity of your business your sales funnel will be different. If you want to scale your company one day this is something you will need.

Giving out discounts

Discounts are like winning lottery tickets, everybody wants one. Any successful entrepreneur will tell you to never lead a pitch offering a discount, but if you must give a discount at least be a little strategic about. Early in my career I broke my discount requests into two categories. Growth projects, which can be defined as a project that adds immense value to your finances, clout, or expertise. A pace project is classified as a project that is neutral. These are usually projects that are small in dollar amount, but allow you to pay bills and have little or no negative impact on you other than loss of time. As I became a more in demand creative I quickly adopted only dealing with potential clients that were only willing and able to purchase services. Keywords being willing and able. In classic economic style I transitioned from giving discounts to not giving them at all. You will spend more time trying to convince someone your worth than working with the clients that see your true value. This method is not for the faint of hearts. You will lose potential revenue at first, but it's totally worth it in the end. Part of giving discounts is knowing when to stop. Not every project deserves a discount, and again, you should never lead with giving discounts.

Early Career discounting:

•When you want to gain access or knowledge

•If you can afford to

•To build relationships

•If it is work for charity or a great cause

Don't fall for it:

Too often we give discounts because someone promises us more work. When the client doesn't hold up their end of the bargain we are often left hanging dry wishing we charged them full price. The best way to combat this is asking for full price for the initial project and giving discounts based on the amount of future projects.

Overall discounts shouldn't be looked at as an initial response nor should they be looked at as last resorts. Use discounts as tools and use them wisely.

It really does take money to make money

Finding ways to fund my ambitions have never been difficult to me. I have collected aluminium cans to buy paintbrushes and have cut hair to start a t-shirt line. These days there are plenty of authors and bloggers who will tell the story of the lean, mean start-up. They will paint the picture of a solely independent shop that bootstrapped funds to make their dreams come true. In my case, I didn't even have the boots, let alone the straps. So working a 9 to 5 job was the only way I was going to fund my entrepreneurial ventures. I knew using the company I worked for to catapult my creative endeavours was equal to them using me to increase their bottom line. Some individuals don't see it this way. They are blinded by the benefits, comfort, and paid time off. In reality, this method is just business; companies want to maximize profits and minimize cost. Companies do this by hiring you, instead outsourcing you. This all justified me using their resources to help me. With that being said, you're out of your mind if you think a 9 to 5 will render you financial freedom. Unless you have a rich family willing to support you financially as an emerging creative, you will need a source of income. For the same reasons architects don't cut corners when designing homes, you shouldn't cut corners when it comes to investing in your creative ventures. Spend money on a good web site, save up for conferences, and pay for memberships into creative organizations and the list goes on. Do you need a lot of money? No. But you will need some money. Remember being cheap can be expensive. So don't quit your day job just yet.

Never say I can't

From the time I was a child I was always taught if you can't do something, find someone who can. This principle of life has carried me a long way, especially in the creative business. When I first started my agency, eighty percent of the services I offered, we weren't able to do. That didn't stop us. Nor did it matter. Even though I had no clue how to code a website, I had friends that could code a website at high levels. Let's say I didn't know anyone that could code, there are plenty of websites that offer this freelance service by the boatload. With websites like Fiverr.com and Upwork.com, there is no excuse for you to be saying "I can't" unless you're saying that to cheap potential clients who are trying to low ball you. Compile a list of your peers and try to get a current price range of their services, that way you have quicker responses to quotes and requests for proposals (rfps). Outsourcing work to more experienced contractors alleviates workload and stress, and who doesn't want that. Just make sure they do great work.

Just do the work.

It's true your biggest billboard will be the ones that walk. It's funny how advertising companies never have their own billboards. You'll never see Weiden & Kennedy take out a thirty-second spot on Fox Network advertising on how good they are in advertising. What you will see is a thirty-second commercial shot by Weiden & Kennedy air during the super bowl. I tell you who else saw that same commercial, potential clients. Creatives don't need to advertise as much as other professions. Our work speaks for itself. You just have to make sure your work says what you want it to say. Most of my clients have come from other clients. In fact, I've never taken out an ad to promote my creative work. So throwing money at your sales problem won't always get you the results you need. The work will always speak for itself.

Show results

In my company's early days we had two restaurants on our client list. Both of these establishments were very young. After taking each company through our discovery process I found that the burger joint needed to improve the quality of its burgers and the breakfast joint needed to expand its menu. The burger joint owner thought I was overreaching by suggesting he change up his menu. We did a survey on what the locals thought about his product. When we confronted the owner with our findings and decided to purchase graphics from us and not worry about the product development we suggested. The breakfast joint expanded their menu and added a rewards system we also suggested they put in place. Today that burger joint is closed and the breakfast joint has two locations and is thinking of opening a third. I like to think we had a part in their tremendous growth. I've always used this example when telling my clients why they should listen to me. That's why created a case study revolved around the success we helped create for the restaurants. It is important for creatives to do case studies on their client, because case studies show the effectiveness of your work. Case studies state the problem a client presented to you, the strategy you implemented to fix that problem, and the results from you fixing the problem. Case studies can serve as a playbook for you when dealing similar issues with future clients. Aside from the structure benefits having case studies can increase your ability to charge more. When potential clients see that your work produces results they are more willing to pay the premium price.

Ways to show results

•Write case studies

•Win awards

•Set key performance indicators prior to project

Example: Likes, shares, sales, traffic, sales

Manage expectations

Before I embark on any project I like to know what my clients expect of me, and more importantly, I like them to know what I expect of them. This initial contact is very crucial to the relationship between the client and you. Too often we get excited about a project and forget to state the expectations of the project. In most cases, after having an initial conversation with a potential client I type out a scope of work that explains all details pertaining to the project. This allows the client to see exactly what I am doing and what I will be delivering. This can be attached to a contract or can be a contract. Not every project requires a contract, but every project does require a scope of work. Sometimes you can put it in a text, e-mail, or letter. Just make sure there is a paper trail of details to cover you and your client's investment. Managing expectations has a lot to do with holding each party accountable for holding up their end of the deal. Letting your clients know in the beginning about your process and procedures allows them to assess how they will navigate the project, which will lead to less stress on the client management side.

Process of Managing Expectations

•*Conference call about the scope of work wanted by the client*

•*A follow up e-mail listing the scope of work along with any other details discussed during the conference call*

•*Official scope/contract attached with a quote*

•*Weekly updates on project details*

Pay your taxes

There's nothing wrong with paying taxes. In fact, being a tax paying citizen has its benefits, and being a tax paying business has even more. When I didn't have enough money to buy a high powered cinema camera for my company I turned to micro-lenders like Accion to help me. One of the first things they asked me was did I have my tax returns from the last three years. It wasn't that they wanted to see the amount I made; they had my bank statements for that. They were looking to prove my company's legitimacy. I got the loan and increased my prices by seventy-five percent; the rest is history. There are many ways, too many to count, on how you can benefit from paying taxes, and they all depend on your situation. The bottom line is, paying taxes keeps you out of trouble and can totally legitimize your creative company.

Save your money

Frugalness came naturally to me. As a child, I saved money because I didn't know when was the next time I was going to get some more. My mother always taught me how to stretch a dollar. Creative entrepreneurs biggest problem is that their biggest asset is that the money can come fast at times. Especially when your seasoned and well connected. When the gigs do come in an abundance creatives shouldn't jump the gun and start splurging on frivolous things. In fact when that time comes the best thing you can do is start saving your money.

Reasons why you should save your money

1. **Bigger Projects.** Most upcoming creatives would kill to get a contract to do a big video for a company for $10,000. When companies are willing to invest this amount of money into their brand in some cases they will pay a net 30. A net30 means the company has 30 days to pay you after your services have been rendered. So you get the opportunity and you want to bring on a bigger film crew or rent a better camera. The problem is, the film crew are not about to wait thirty days to get paid. If you've saved some money, maybe you could pay them a deposit first. At one point my company took on a big film project where we had to travel to three different cities. I knew I had enough money saved to send my team to those cities. Even though expenses were included in the budget, we wouldn't see that money until we got paid at the end of the project. Big projects come

with cost. If you save your money, you can afford to take them on.

2. **Equipment.** Being creative can be expensive, especially when it comes to buying equipment. Save money up for a new camera or computer, or to replace something that breaks. Whatever the case might be, you will always need some cash for equipment.

3. **Networking.** From attending conferences to joining chambers of commerce and other professional organizations, it all costs money. Putting money to the side for these things makes you a better creative entrepreneur and puts you in the right places at the right time. Networking is not free, at least the effective events aren't.

4. **To quit your day job.** The only reason you're still at your job is because of money and maybe health insurance. My goal was to save three times my salary and then I would quit my day job for a part-time one. Overall, you should be doing what

you love to do every day and be making a living doing so.

Put it on Paper

Like I said before in the beginning not every project deserves the energy of a lengthy contract, but when that time comes you need to be ready. When we first started our agency we had no contracts, but we did put all our agreements in email. I don't recommend that now, but we did what we had to do. Contracts are extremely

---

ABOUT CONTRACTS

THEY HOLD ALL PARTIES ACCOUNTABLE
THEY KEEP YOU ON TRACK OF WHAT YOU HAVE TO DELIVER
SOMETIMES YOUR BUSINESS INSURANCE REQUIRES IT
YOU CAN FIND CONTRACTS ON LEGALZOOM OR CONTACT A LAWYER

KREADIV +
KOO

edaiv & Koo LLC Project Scope of Work Contract

ient Name:_____

rimary Contact & Address: _____

_____

Project Name: _____

Contractor: Kreadiv & Koo LLC

~~_____~~

Primary Contact: ~~_____~~

This contract is an offer on _____ for *Contractor* to provide creative *Work* as requested by *Client*.

1. Work

Client requests *Contractor* to create a logo design, develop brand image, and website. *Work* includes the final, deliverable items, and any preliminary *Work, research*, sketches, or other materials created while working on said project. Here is a detailed scope of work schedule we will do for you.

Website Development	Up to 5 pages SEO Optimized Content provided	$4500
Website Maintenance	6 months Content updates Troubleshooting	$1,050
		$5,550
Total Payment		

2. Payment **(NET 30 PAYMENT)**

Initial payment will be 0% of total payment in the amount of

Final Payment is payable within 2 business days of receipt of deliverables (finished goods). The grant of any license or right of copyright is conditioned on receipt of full payment.

3. Estimates

The fees and expenses shown are a maximum limit unless an hourly fee has been agreed upon. That fee will be _____ (50%) and *Contractor* shall provide the *Client* of a tally of hours within a reasonable period of time upon request if such is the measure of the fee not to exceed 10% of the estimated time without approval by the Client. Final fees, itemized accounting of time spent and expenses shall be shown when invoice is rendered.

4. Cancellation

Either party may cancel the contract at any time. If the *Contractor* breaches or cancels the cont[ract] fee based project, all fees paid for the project will be refunded to the *Client* within 30 days. If the *Contractor* breaches or cancels the contract for hourly based work, any fees already paid for unf[inished] work will be refunded or hourly fees due will be canceled. Fees will be refunded or paid within 30 [days. If the] *Client* cancels or breaches the contract, all hourly work to date will be paid and ownership of all copyrights and the original materials shall be retained by the *Contractor*.

5. We have agreed on the plan and you have signed off on it. Now we set the time schedu[le] and priorities. Once these are approved, we will move into execution.

In the case of creative work we will first develop a "Creative Strategy" for each project. Th[is] clearly define what you and we expect the work to accomplish, against what target, and th[e] thought to be communicated.

6. Schedule of Approvals

Each client is granted 3 free revisions of each individual project. The client will receive periodically updates from staff and creative in order to ensure that process goes smoothly:

7. Deadlines

All deadlines are agreed upon and set by clients and company. To better help clients we have created a table to help schedule revisions and deliverables based on workloads.

5-Day Work Schedule	10 –Day Work Schedule	15-Day Work Schedule	20-Day Work Schedule
Day 2- Revision 1	Day 3- Revision 1	Day 5- Revision 1	Day 8- Revision 1
Day 3- Revision 2 & 3	Day 6- Revision 2	Day 10 - Revision 2	Day 12- Revision 2
Day 4- Finalization	Day 8- Revision 3	Day 13- Revision 3	Day 16- Revision 3
Day 5- Delivered	Day 9- Finalization	Day 14- Finalization	Day 19- Finalization
	Day 10- Delivered	Day 15- Delivered	Day 20- Delivered
Associated Work	Associated Work	Associated Work	Associated Work
Simple Logos	Websites	Websites	Database Websites
Stationary Design	Complex Logos	Complex Logos	Brand management
Blog design	Digital Branding	Content marketing	Creative Event Plans
Brand Consulting	Extreme Ads	Digital Marketing	Logo Packages
Ad Design	Commercials	SEO, SEM,	Social Media Marketing

By Signing this document you have agreed to the terms of work stated above.

CLIENT SIGNATURES _____

CONTRACTOR SIGNATURES _____ DATE _____

DATE _____

Resources

Starting a Business:
EIN: www.irs.gov
DBA: Local tax office or courthouse
LLC: www.legalzoom.com
Websites: Envato Hosted (Wordpress prefered)

Organizations that offer help:
Small Business Development Centers
Chamber of Commerce
Economic Development Centers
Women Business Center

Submit for Awards:
AMA Crystal Awards
Hermes Creative Awards
Cannes Lions
CLIO Awards
ADDY Awards
Effie Awards
D&AD Awards

Microlenders:
Accion
Kiva
Lift Fund
Opportuntity Fund

6

Creative Muscle

Chapter 6

Creativity is like a muscle, if you don't use it you might lose it. Whether it's writing, acting, debating, or filming, you have to constantly training. Throughout my career I have sought out challenges to strengthen my abilities as a creative. I took on programs that I had no clue about, and picked up books I wouldn't normally read.

The world is full of creative and extraordinary people who can think at high levels. The world's best companies know this, and they are continually trying to crack the code of high volume creativity. You see it all the time with tech companies, with their offices full of pool tables and public video game stations, or rooms covered in dry erase boards. They are willing to do anything to cultivate the fresh energy that generates great ideas. The truth is, ideas don't always come when you want them to, and the goods ones rarely show up at all. For me personally, my creativity always came from the simple things in my everyday life.

Read, and drink more water

I'm a firm believer that drinking more water helps everything. Besides water, reading a few books doesn't hurt either. Some of the best practical advice is hidden in books. I'm often reading more than one book at time. I do this for two reasons. One, because I get bored easily. Two, because I'm often reading about the same subject, I like comparing different perspectives from each book. We all know reading is fundamental, but it also can be instrumental in your growth as a creative. For the most part, authors usually take their time crafting well thought out content that can really be beneficial to their readers, while bloggers are charged with putting out content at a more rapid pace that causes them to sometimes overlook the finer details. This is to not discredit blogs; there are a few of them with very reliable content. But as a creative, you cannot omit the power of a good book. What you read is solely based on you and the situation you are in. I'll admit I never had a problem reading; I just never got into fiction. I only wanted to read real stories. Reading a book to its end shouldn't always be a task, especially if you're trying learn from it. It should be a journey you take on your own. I sometimes read books backwards, or skip over chapters. I do whatever it takes to keep me engaged and informed. I'm a firm believer that books should inform, reveal, or inspire. Books are important, and you would be doing your creative career a disservice if you never picked one up. But if you're reading this you obviously get the point.

Learn Photoshop

No matter what type of creative you are, I believe you should know Photoshop. I believe in the future it will be one of those programs you're just going to have to know, like Microsoft Word. You don't have to become an expert, but getting familiar with the program definitely won't hurt your career. Learning a software as complex as Photoshop sharpens your critical thinking skills, enables you to save money on the outsourcing of simple design work, and adds to your arsenal of tools. I always encouraged my colleagues to learn Photoshop, even though I was the designer in the department. It not only freed me of the monotonous simple tasks, it also allowed the company I worked for to enhance its efficiency. Social media planners no longer had to wait on me for simple post graphics, writers could design their own layouts, and cinematographers could create simple lower thirds. When I was getting ready to graduate college, nearly all the marketing positions I applied for asked if I knew Photoshop. Lucky for me, I did. Employers are demanding more out of creatives, it's no longer competitive to be solely focused on one tool to be successful. Learning Photoshop is easier than you think, and with so many YouTube tutorials available there is no excuse not to.

Pick up a number 2: analogue vs. digital

The term "Out with the old and in with the new" has no place in the creative world. The curator in me won't allow me to destroy old relics I deem valuable. In other words, my wife thinks I'm a hoarder. She couldn't be farther from the truth. Truth is, I have benefited from doing things the analogue way and the digital way. Creating things is far easier when you have the best of both worlds to work with.

In this digital age no one ever handwrites anymore, and even when they do, it's with either a mechanical pencil or some brand pen. In fact, as I write out the rough draft of this manuscript my utensil of choice is a ball point ink pen. So when is it all right to take it back and pick up a number 2 pencil? The answer to that is, always. You can't manufacture creativity, so sparking creativity becomes an effort when you need to do it on a regular basis. Using a number 2 pencil gives me nostalgic memories which often lead to inspirations and effective brainstorming.

Whether its sketching ideas or writing notes in my notebook, grasping a fresh cut pencil always signifies endless possibilities for me. To a writer this might not mean picking up a pencil, it might mean using a typewriter. To a photographer, this might mean picking up a Polaroid camera. Nostalgic pieces always seem to spark my youthful memories and give me great ideas. I'm not saying give up your laptop for an old gateway. I am saying don't be quick to throw away old things or try old things every once in a while. You never know when something old might spark something new.

Evolving

In 1969 President Eisenhower formed the Advanced Research Project Agency (ARPA). This agency was tasked with creating a form of communication that could endure a nuclear attack. The anxiety and paranoia the Cold War caused in America was met with all kind of government funded experiments. That same paranoia led the many great minds at ARPA to create the first digital message. On October 29, 1969 a computer from UCLA transmitted a message to a computer at Stanford. That technology would later be called the Internet. When the dot com boom begin to happen in the mid 90's people all over begin to use the internet in ways you couldn't fathom. The internet had grew from a military project into world necessity.

Just like the evolution of the internet you too must evolve. How will you evolve as a creative? The problem is, some creatives don't like change and they resist the natural evolution of a creative. The time of learning new things that keeps them from conforming. These individuals fail to keep up with new trends and technology to do their job. They distance themselves from growth opportunities and new ways of thinking.

Years back I had the pleasure of sitting on a selection committee to hire several graphic designers. This process is far from short.

"**STOP** COMPLAINING ABOUT WHAT YOU DONT **HAVE** AND GET STUFF **DONE.**"

Surprisingly, only one candidate met the design requirements we needed to fulfil the position. It wasn't that the other candidates didn't have experience; in fact one candidate had over twenty years of experience. It wasn't the fact that their design work sucked. The thing that discouraged the selection committee the most was that the undesirable candidate's portfolio showed no growth from inception to end. The candidate had been doing the same type of work for twenty plus years, never showing diversity or growth in their skill set.

Often when you embrace your evolution you pick up things you never thought you would be interested in. In 2006 all I wanted to do was pain and sketch. A couple years later I learned about Photoshop and graphic design as a whole. By 2011 I had picked up photography, and cinematography came shortly after. By 2015 I was fully immersed in writing and digital strategy, I didn't plan on picking up a camera, nor did I plan on embarking in strategy, I just wanted to create ads for magazines. But as an active creative, the new information was constantly presenting itself and that innate feeling to create took over every time. The new skills I picked up made my designs better and my perspective richer. Don't fight the natural progression in you as a creative; doing so can hinder you in the long run.

Exercise

As painful as it sounds, putting yourself through a killer workout can spark the fire you need to get your creativity boiling. We all know for certain that staring a computer screen never helped anyone's creativity! So if you need to create something, go get your body moving. Besides the physical health benefits of working out, exercise has always helped me mentally as well. When I first started working out, it was solely to lose weight and keep my doctor happy. Then I slowly began to realize how much more productive I had become. Even though I am not at the physical shape I hope to be, my mental health has improved tremendously from exercising more regularly.

Keep a journal

I received my first journal from my mom on Christmas Day, 2004. It was pretty much the only thing she could afford to get me for Christmas, and I still write in that same journal to this very day. Now I have at least seven journals, all of them serving the same purpose: to record my creativity. When I have an idea, I go to my journals. When I take meetings, I write notes in my journal. We are not computers, so we have to write down our big spontaneous ideas as they come to us—otherwise, we might lose them. Keeping a journal saved my life. When I was dealing with plight of the world I could always escape inside my journal. Write!

Find your purpose

I believe art should be accessible to anyone who wants to participate in it. It shouldn't be reserved for the rich or privilege. When I realized that I was part of group of people that were purposefully being left out of the creative industry I quickly begin to study the history of this problem. I wanted to know why were there so many black people not getting jobs in advertising or marketing. It bothered me so much that our stories weren't being told right. I researched and researched until I realized that no one could tell me the answer to this problem. It was then, when I dedicated my creative career and life to help create opportunities for creatives of color. Pastor Mike Todd once said, "God is not committed to your dreams, he is committed to his purpose for your life." When you have a purpose, it easy to sit back and let it drive your creativity. When you find your purpose, you are no longer in control; your dreams are then on autopilot. A lot of creatives seem everywhere in their ideas and scattered in their focus, and that is because their trying live their dreams and not their purpose. Amongst the many uses of creativity, I believe one of its core abilities is to be a vehicle for change. Purpose is what drove the creativity of our Civil Rights Leaders, which eventually got Lyndon B. Johnson to pass the Civil Rights Act of 1964. Purpose is what drove the creativity behind Dorothy Zeller's iconic Black Panther party logo. Creativity needs a purpose, and purpose requires creativity. When I chose to let my purpose drive, everything else in my life got better.

 ## Try listening to music

Just like purpose, music can drive your creativity to new heights. There is nothing like listening to a slow R&B mix while painting, or writing a blog while playing some trap music. When an artist asks me to design a cover, I automatically ask for their music to get some inspiration—because I never want to create artwork that doesn't match the music. Music might be that creative edge you need to push out work when its crunch time, so don't hesitate to snap on your headphones.

Make sure your mental health is good

I would be remiss if I didn't expound on the importance of mental health. As black people, in general, we go through so much. Just because you have God-given creative abilities doesn't mean you are exempt from the struggles of being black. Being happy mentally makes for good creative work. Often we as black creatives feel like no one understands us, and this might be true sometimes. Finding someone to talk to—or someone who can educate you on dealing with mental issues—can improve your creativity tenfold. I had been putting off seeing a therapist for so long, until one day, I just decided enough was enough. Seeing a therapist helped me unpack 20 years of clutter in my mind. It was so worth the time and the money to have someone to talk to professionally. If you can't find an affordable therapist, find someone to talk to who you can trust. Find someone who can relate to you. I healthy mind goes along way.

Simple things creatives should learn

Basic Photographer

Creative Writing

Update a WordPress site

Brainstorming

Event Planning

Social media Ad Buying

Storyboard

Present an Idea

7

Time Management

Chapter 7

Time is the most precious known commodity to man, but yet we waste it like it's in abundance. When I decided to start my agency I knew had no money, but also realized I had a lot of time. So while working a 9 to 5 I decided to spend at least 3 hours a day working on my business. When I couldn't afford something my business needed I spent time learning how to do that very thing. When I needed a high-end website to showcase my work I spent time learning how to build one. When I couldn't afford a film crew I spent time teaching myself how to work a cinema cameras, and the list goes on. Besides using your time as a substitute of money, taking actionable steps to stop wasting time is also important.

Not everybody deserves a meeting

When trying to get new business you will find yourself arranging meetings with just about everybody. The rush of getting a new client with a new project is like the day before school starts and you've got new clothes. The phone calls from potential new clients not only scream money, but they are indicators that you're heading in the right direction. I receive e-mails, calls, and pop ups of potential clients wanting to meet for an initial consultation just about every day. It's time to be more selective on whom you meet with.

A couple of ways I avoid unnecessary meetings

1. First, have some constraint. If your calendar is filled, don't take on any unnecessary meetings if don't have time. The quickest way to creative fatigue is to overextend yourself.

Lose the trinkets

We tend to hold onto material things like trinkets, and these trinkets cause us to lose confidence when we thought they were supposed to help us gain it. The more stuff you have, the more stuff you are able to lose. When you finally get enough money to get yourself a car, house, and an occasional trip, you are afraid to lose those little trinkets you worked for. We all do it; we become slaves to the assets we worked so hard for. I'm not saying it's wrong to have nice things, I myself have nice things. I'm only saying, don't let the things you work hard for cripple your decision making or distract you.

In some cases, losing trinkets physically is less important than losing them mentally. The problem arises when you rely on material things to build your confidence and eventually dictate your creativity. If you're in the business of creativity, anxiety from losing material things isn't healthy for your bottom line, and being fearless and innovative only helps. Losing trinkets is not just about material things, it's also about mental things. The most important thing for a creative is a free mind. Your time should be spent creating dope work, not taking on projects just to pay bills that you can don't need.

It's ok to throw in the towel

One of my biggest lessons in life came when I decided to end my festival. After 3 years of throwing the event and not making a profit it was time to throw in the towel. Although we had received great press and word of mouth, the ticket sales weren't where we wanted them to be. After the second festival I told myself "Hey, this is the last one," but the people around encouraged me to keep the ball rolling and so, with hesitation, we began to plan our third Space City Food Truck

Festival. This time things were different. The team I had started with didn't seem as enthused as they had been, and their mood rubbed off on me. I got frustrated with their work ethic and lack of sense of urgency. I started to feel like I was on an island by myself. Running the festival no longer felt like fun. I even threatened to cancel the whole thing twice. Then I decided this would be the last time I did the festival. I cut my losses and threw in the towel. I don't regret doing the festival, the marketing we did for it won my agency several awards. Though the time I spent on the festival could have been spent on growing my agency, I did gain a lot of experience in throwing large events. I bit off more than I could chew, and I had to accept that. If you have a gut feeling that what you are doing might not be for you, go with it, keeping in mind it doesn't necessarily mean giving up. It could mean taking a break or moving in another direction.

Is it time to quit?

•If you're not having fun anymore.

•If it's hurting you more than its helping you.

•If you physically can't do it.

•When you have a better idea.

•If you're losing money consistently.

Don't get distracted by material things, avoid meaningless meetings, and it's okay to take a break on things that aren't working for you.

Organization

Now I'll be the first to admit that I'm not the most organized person, but I would be doing you a disservice if I didn't let you know how important it is. In the beginning, when you barely have clients and the projects aren't very demanding, you can survive without being very organized. In a perfect world, you can have a bunch of clients and still maintain the simple and free structure you had when you first started, you can't have your cake and eat it too. When your business grows from having three clients a month to ten clients a month, you will have to change the way you manage your work flow. When your business grows from $1,200 a month to $6,000 a month, you will have to change your accounting system. Here are some tools and tactics I have used to help make running my creative business much easier.

GET ORGANIZED

Team Collaboration

Basecamp

Slack App

GroupMe

Facebook Groups

Google Docs

Financials

Your Bank App

QuickBooks

Stripe Payment

PayPal

Cash App

TurboTax

Log Mileage

Planning

Google Calendar

White Dry Erase Boards

Phone Reminders

Note Planners

Inventory

Square POS

Shelves with Labels

Boxes with Labels

Excel Sheet with Inventory

Quantity

Year It Was Built

Cost

Serial Number

Excuses

When I pitch new business or present to clients I already have two strikes against me. I'm young and black. Older executives often assume I lack experience, while other others assume I lack competence. Both assumptions couldn't be further from the truth. I realized this stigma was something that I had to overcome in order to excel. When I first meet someone who is eager to join my team, I explain to them in as much detail as possible about how much I dislike excuses. A lot of time when creatives meet each other there is this a great exchange of excitement and energy, and everyone wants to be best friends and start creating together—but if you want to be successful in this business, you have to dial that back and manage your expectations. Let the people around you know that excuses are not welcome in your circle. You might come off really mean to some people, but for some people this might be exactly what they need to hear. When you're in this line of work, excuses can cost you a lot of money—or they can mean you're out of business entirely.

I have always demanded my interns to be very upfront with me; if they couldn't do something or didn't know how to do something, they should let me know right away. My uncle taught me to just get the job done no matter what, and I believe that mentality has served as an advantage for me. Now I'm not saying you have to be perfect, but you do have to be consistent. In the past I've stopped using many designers and filmmakers because they gave me too many excuses why they couldn't meet deadlines, etc.

• *Manage expectations; if you can't do something, say it. Leaving people hanging until the last minute can cause distrust.*

• *Don't blame your mistakes on someone else; accept it and move on.*

• *Clients don't care about excuses; they want results and so should you.*

• *Some excuses are not excuses, they are emergencies.*

8

Some Super Practical
Advice

Chapter 8

"Every creative needs a website."

Some advice is common sense and some advice you might have to hear every day. Some advice doesn't deserve analogies or short stories to reinforce the theories that accompany them. Over the years I have consumed little nuggets of wisdom from people of all shades and ages. The simple but useful advice given by these individuals have help propel my career. This advice is also too important for you not to have it.

You still need a physical portfolio.

Designer Faith Wang stated, "Print portfolios have been the standard method of presenting work for years, but the digital age has emphasized the need for designers to have an internet presence... so it is important to provide multiple complete and well-maintained options to present your work." I believe this is extremely true. When I was searching for employment I always made sure I had a physical portfolio. In a lot of cases I would be the only candidate showing up with a portfolio, especially if the company didn't recommend you bring one. In some cases companies just wanted you to send them a link to your online portfolio. So I suppose I was over doing it, but there is nothing like having a physical copy of your work. The feel of quality paper and binding always enhances a viewer's senses and lets them know your serious and prepared.

One of the steps I made was order a custom wooden portfolio binding with my initials carved in it. It was expensive, but well worth the eyes it garnered. The industry is so competitive, and you're going to need whatever edge you can get. Physical portfolios are not obsolete, they are imperative to your competiveness and visibility. I know you're saying, "What if I'm a videographer or writer?" If you are in those professions, having a physical portfolio can really set you apart. Some of the ways a videographer can use a portfolio is map out their process , show shooting angle graphs, still photos from films they've shot, list equipment they use and other behind the scenes details people want to know. A writer can show the content they've written along with the cover of the magazine or a screen shot of the website the article was featured on. This type of attention to details and content will set you apart.

You don't have to build a site from scratch.

In the retail industry, it's all about location. The same goes for the creativity industry, and the best location for a business these days is the internet. Every creative needs a website. Not everyone will look at it, but it's like one of those just in case things. Some people think having a website is obsolete suggesting that social media as a better option. Their view is jaded. Social media are tools; your website should be the center of operations. Your social media should always point to your website, or hosted site. Creating a website doesn't have to be expensive, but quality does matter. Most of the time your website will serve as a filter system for the type of clients you want. I learned this from Rick Webb's book, Agency. If your site looks cheap, chances are you will either get cheap clients or no clients at all. If your site looks expensive, most of the time you will get serious clients willing to spend some serious money. Whatever you do, just make sure you have a website. The first thing I do when someone comes up to me after a speaking engagement is ask them if they have a site. You would be surprised the number of creatives I meet who don't have a site. It's too important to leave out.

Art is a contact sport

In this industry, people can be cannibalistic. At the first sight of weakness, neighbouring creatives will try to discredit and smear your name. People will say they want to collaborate and even make false attempts to collaborate just to get close to you. As a creative, you have to understand that this is an industry that everyone wants to be in and everyone is struggling to stay in. Grasping this realization makes you less vulnerable to malicious behaviour. I have seen ideas stolen, contracts cancelled, promises not fulfilled and even worse cases of physical altercations between creatives. You've got to protect your energy in a very diplomatic way. I have always paid close attention to the industry people I attached myself to.

Customer service and experience is important

In reflecting on why he was the first black-owned automobile company to reach one billion dollars in sales, Greg Jackson once stated, "Customer service is the hallmark of any business." This is extremely true. As good as it sounds, you're not the only one selling a creative service. So if we have the same product or service as someone else, the only thing that can set us apart from the competition is the service we give our customers. Mr. Jackson also stated that in his business "The customer is always right," and when it comes to selling cars, he might be right. We are not selling cars; we are selling something much more complex.

When I started shooting wedding films I quickly realized that it wasn't my customer service I needed to improve, it was my customer experience. I was always polite to my clients, I gave them several payment options, I was always on time, etc.; those were basics of customer service. Customer experience is more about the journey your client takes with your brand, while as customer service is more about the assistance a brand gives its customers. So in order to improve my customer experience, I had to make my website more responsive to all communication devices, meet in person more with clients and walk them through the process and gave them a flash drive with their raw wedding footage on it. With the enhancement to my customer experience, I quickly saw referrals and bookings go up.

In the big picture, customer service is an important part of the customer experience, but at most, it is used when something goes wrong with the customer. This is something creatives fail to think about. Forbes stated, "Customer experience is more than just a buzzword—it should be at the heart of everything a company does. By including customer service and customer care, brands can exceed expectations and delight customers. In other words before you start selling your paintings, or creating graphics, think about the customer experience.

Don't let your job hinder you from being creative.

The creative industry is cutthroat; the creative workplace has even more dead bodies. Through my several jobs as designer I always held onto my creative edge no matter how monotonous the work got or how confusing the direction was.

Your job is a tool and if you want to eventually work for yourself you should be working on an exit strategy. Learn as much as you can from your job, build relationships with the people there.

The relationship with your job should be one of mutual benefits. If and when that relationship is not a benefiting you start searching for a way out. Don't burn bridges when exiting a company. You never know when you will need your old boss for a reference.

Certifications can help

Having certifications doesn't guarantee you will get business, but not having them can hinder you from getting them. In some cases, having certifications will be the reason you don't get invited to bids or vendor tradeshows. Working at the Small Business Development Center I learned the importance of having certain certifications under the tutelage of Bridgett Ross. During my time at the center we signed up minority businesses with the HUB Certification. HUB meaning Historically Underutilized Business was a certification designed to give minority owned businesses a fair shot at government contracts. When I decided to get a certification in SEO (Search Engine Optimization), I did it to show my peers and my potential clients that I was well qualified. Although sometimes getting certifications can take time, the financial rewards can outweigh the cost.

Why Certifications are Important

- *They give you more opportunity*
- *Keeps you current on new techniques, trends, and information in your industry*
- *Helps with getting hired*
- *Helps with becoming a thought leader*

Embrace technology and data

Naturally, we are makers. We like to use our hands to mold the things we are dreaming about. We like to focus on the creative side and not on the information that might drive those creative decisions. With new technology emerging in the creative industry every day, we either get on board or we get left behind. Many other creatives are marrying data they get from marketing tech with their artistic abilities, and they are rendering great results for their clients. And yet, even with all this change, it seems like sometimes the only software we want to pick up is Adobe Suite. Ivana Atlija wrote an article for Digital Agency Network, stating, "Rather than deciding which should drive the other, we must allow data and creative to work in tandem with one another. It's not about picking favorites, it's about maintaining balance." She couldn't be more correct. I believe that when welcome technology into our creative process, things can become more efficient and we make better work.

Chapter 9

When I graduated from college, I applied for 128 creative agency jobs and no one called back or even gave me a shot at an internship. For the past several years, that incidence has been the driving force behind my creative intentions. The creative economy has left out people of color for decades, and only a handful of people seem to really care. Citylab.com did a study and found that almost 73.8 percent of creative jobs were held by white people. This problem is nothing new. Beginning in late 2008 the NAACP had a full on legal assault against the advertising industry called the Madison Avenue Projects for the industry's biased hiring practices.

The NAACP called out some huge brands for
not hiring agencies that lacked diversity on their
creative teams. Dating back even further there
has always been diversity and inclusion problems
within creative careers. One might ask why, but
that would be a rhetorical question or insult. The
truth is, we are just as creative and able to compete
with our on-black counterparts.

Make no mistake; this problem is ours to fix and no
one else's. We have to demand our beloved brands
to spend with our multicultural owned agencies
or hire more creatives of color. We have to create
an education pipeline that informs our creative
students of the endless creative possibilities. Some
of our HBCUs will have to update curriculum that
makes students more competitive in the workforce.
A part of the problem is that we are expecting the
government to step in with rules and regulations,
or we expect a chief diversity officer to change
a company's culture overnight. Creatives of all
spectrums must be on board with this initiative.
Diversity has to be intentional. We can no longer

sit on the side-lines and wait on to be included. We have to create actionable plans that render measurable results. If that means creating more programs like Lincoln Stephens's Marcus Graham Project out of Dallas, Texas, then so be it. Lincoln's idea of industry sponsored advertising boot camp came into fruition in 2008. The program takes a group of creatives of color and places them in real-life agency situations while building their network. His program has enabled many of his participants to gain employment within the creative industry. Programs like his and several other ones need our support and need to be duplicated in other cities. Knowing the problem exists is no longer enough; we have to have solutions.

Education is a key

I don't mean a formal one, either. If you're like me, chances are you never heard of portfolio school or advertising school. Schools like Miami Ad School, Creative Circus and Parsons exist to get you jobs in advertising, photography and film. Most of the time, these types schools have relationships with agencies and industry leaders, because they too employee industry leaders to teach in their classes. Students get a chance to build portfolios that agencies actually want. For some reason, black people just don't know about these types of schools or don't have chances to enroll due to the time demand and financial burden schools place on their students. We know about the many traditional forms of higher education, but we don't know about schools that are literally created to get you a job in the industry. Tech, fashion, entertainment companies, etc., attend semester portfolio reviews at these institutions and hire students on the spot. These students then work for large agencies until one of the clients offer them three times their salary to do freelance work. Those guys usually end up starting their own agency with a top brand in their pocket and hire more students that look like them. And the pipeline continues. As simple as I put that, this combination of nepotism, privilege, and racism runs deep. At the surface level creative education has to be more affordable and accessible to people of color.

I believe that HBCU's have a clear advantage to create a pipeline to the creative industry.

1. Institutions have update curriculum that is relevant to the creative jobs that are current and have to be more flexible to adapt to the future trends of the creative workforce. Hire more professors with real life experience and who have ties to the industry.

2. University must create relationships with agencies and companies. In some cases, universities aim for the low hanging fruit by only building relations with companies with large alumni populations. Colleges will have to foster more challenging relationships with agencies and companies. Many of these companies don't have a clue about the amount of talent in HBCU'S.

3. Students will have to demand scholarships to take domestic internships which are often the best ones.

There is nothing more discouraging than landing an internship and find out it's in another city, and you have no money to relocate for three months. Alumni should be giving back for this specific reason.

Selfish Mentality

Aside from lack diversity, one of the main things holding black creatives back is ourselves. We don't collaborate enough, we don't mentor enough, and we don't share enough with each other. The advice I am sharing in this book might not be the best advice for you, and some people may not find this information useful, but it is my attempt to reach back. Reaching back and helping other creatives accomplish their goals should be on everyone's to do list. The selfish mentality must not flourish in creative communities. Instead of being intimidated by another person's success, congratulate them and ask for their advice. Instead of neglecting someone's attempt to ask for advice, show them the path you took. What another person eats, won't make you sick. When another person grows, you can too.

Who's Who

Five years ago when I started my agency, I started researching different black creatives that came before me. This process led me down a black hole of creativity—literally. While I was searching, I discovered black advertising pioneers like Vince Cullers. Cullers started the first advertising company in the United States that marketed toward black consumers in 1956. He was fresh out of design school when he went looking for a job, and he knocked on every agency's door in Chicago. He found out pretty quickly that no one hired black designers, and after he decided he'd had enough rejection, he started his own agency. Finding his story gave me the spark I needed to start my company. It's important that we know the creatives who came before us. Not only are there blueprints of success hidden in their stories, but it's only right that we pay homage. Like I said before, nothing is new under the sun. So who is your who's who?

The Why

We have to control our narrative. We can no longer settle for loosely based depictions of our society. It's no longer acceptable to hire black people for black slaves and not hire black people for the roles of kings and queens of Egypt. Charles S. Dutton wrote, "People tend to work with the same people they've worked with for 20 years. A director hires a director of photography he already knows; the DP hires a cameraman he knows, the cameraman knows a camera operator, and so on. These are the relationships these people have. You can't argue with that." Dutton also said "Don't do a black story and have the gall not to hire any black people." For too long, black stories have been told by people who aren't black—or by people who just aren't in tune with our culture. This causes so much backlash within our community, especially when movies and commercials portray as us nothing more than stereotypes. Being a black creative is more important than ever. Writing our own stories, advertising our own products, building our own buildings, etc. are now just as important as becoming doctors and lawyers.

Overall, we can control our narrative by making conscious decisions to:

•*Speak up for negative and false portrayals of our stories.*
•*Create more accurate content.*
•*Strive for creative leadership roles within corporate America.*
•*Support the stories that depict our culture accurately.*
•*Hire more creatives of color.*

Go Home

"If the educated Negro could go off and be white, he might be happy. The large majority of this class then must go through life denouncing white people because they are trying to run away from the blacks and decrying the blacks because they are not white." So said Carter G. Woodson in The Mis-Education of the Negro. A lot us grew up in places that bring us so many negative thoughts that we simply never go back. I didn't meet my first black designer until I became one. To say that I was the first African American designer from Texarkana, Texas, probably would false—but if there were any, I never met them, nor did they ever come to my school. I never saw a designer during career day, period. There were football and basketball camps, but no art programs. It's simple: if little black kids don't see the arts as a viable way out the hood, then they won't choose that path. That's why it's absolutely imperative for us to go back to our communities and show children that being a graphic designer or a writer can grant you a ticket out. And once we get out, we must create culture of giving back—not just in money, but in time and energy.

Nuture Creativity

I was a first-generation college student in my household, and only a handful people in my entire family to graduate college. When I decided I wanted to go college, I knew I lacked a reliable blueprint for how to get there. When I discovered my inherent artistic abilities, I knew I had to follow them. Thankfully my mother knew I was great at art, but she didn't know what to do with it. She didn't know anyone who had made a living from art, nor did she have any resources to help me accomplish any of my creative ambitions at the time. Now that I am a father myself, I realize there were some things she could have done to help me along, and some things she did without knowing that allowed me to explore my creativity. I don't regret my upbringing, mind you. It clearly made me stronger and more resilient. If you have a kid (or know a kid) that might have creative abilities, it's best to foster them as soon as you can.

Recognize curiosity over mischief. My mother understood early on that I wasn't a mischievous child; I was just very, very curious. I was always looking for things to take apart and put back together, especially VCRs. I would always wonder off into the woods to find some old junk that I could dismantle and dissect. Looking back, as along as my mother knew where I was, she really didn't have a problem with my little adventures. Did I get in trouble sometimes? Of course! I never felt like it was for being mischievous, only for not following directions. If we recognize that our children naturally thirst for new things, we can create more opportunities for them to discover things that will keep them engaged and inspired.

Gifted & Talented. Our school had a PTA art contest when I was growing up, and every year from 7th to 11th grade, I always placed either 1st or 2nd in the competition. I was drawing real-life portraits of people by the 6th grade, and by the 8th grade I had found out how create detailed blueprints in Microsoft Paint. I'm not trying to toot my own horn here, but I was clearly gifted and talented from a young age. The school I went to didn't see it that way, though—and for years after it bothered me that I was never in the special classes for gifted students. I also think my average grades might have been part of the reason why I was never selected, but good grades are not the same thing as raw talent and untapped potential. Getting your child into gifted and talented classes might help harness the talent they have early on, so make it a priority if you can.

Invest. Buy paint, go all out on science and art projects, pay for art classes, and take your child to museums. A big part of cultivating that natural talent your kid might have is investing things that they might not be interested in tomorrow. I have purchased cameras, comic books, and art supplies just to see my son use them once. Whatever I can do to spark a child's creative I will do.

Closing

When I decided to write this book, I knew I didn't have all the knowledge, but I knew I wanted to help creatives that looked like me and faced the same problems as me. I knew I didn't have all the answers, but the answers I did have I didn't want to die with me. I wise person once told me that everyone should write the book they wanted to read 10 years ago. Here is my book. Here is a piece of my heart, blood, sweat and tears wrapped in paper and forged in binding. I hope you have found this piece of literature useful, purposeful, and actionable. I encourage you not to wait till your some successful art collector, or millionaire movie director. Where you are now, someone wants to be.

About the Author

Marketer by trade, designer by heart, and entrepreneur by default. Michael Todd Thomas Jr. is the creative director and founder of **Kreadiv & Koo Agency**, a full-service marketing and branding agency for education and purpose-based institutions.

Michael is an advocate for diversity and inclusion in the creative industry, creating events that focus on providing creatives of color tips, resources, and opportunities. He is also the co-creator of the Annual **Space City Food Truck Festival**, one of Houston's Top music and food truck festival. A mentor and speaker to creative entrepreneurs, his talent has won him praise by **American Marketing Association, Association of Excellence,** and **Communicator Awards.**

Born in Texarkana, Texas, lives and works in the Greater Houston Area, and is a graduate of the **Prairie View A&M University,** where he earned his bachelors in marketing and certification in entrepreneurship. He is married with two children, a boy and a girl.

Further Reading

What Makes the Great Great
by Dennis Kimbro

"Part vocational pep rally, part how-to book, What Makes the Great Great elaborates on the inspiring message bestselling author Dennis Kimbro put forth in his first book Think and Grow Rich–A Black Choice. In What Makes the Great Great, the author explores the strategies and thought processes of successful African-Americans." - Dennis Kimbro

Agency: Starting a Creative Firm in the Age of Digital Marketing
by Rick Webb

"This book is for young startups and entrepreneurs in the advertising, marketing, and digital services space. It's an A-to-Z guide for young advertising firms, full of advice that ranges from getting funding to how to value the company and sell it to how to hire your first employee." -Rick Webb

Madison Avenue and the Color Line: African Americans in the Advertising Industry
by Jason Chambers

"Until now, most works on the history of African Americans in advertising have focused on the depiction of blacks in advertisements. As the first comprehensive examination of African American participation in the industry, Madison Avenue and the Color Line breaks new ground by examining the history of black advertising employees and agency owners." - Jason Chambers

Think and Grow Rich: A Black Choice
by Dennis Kimbro

"Author and entrepreneur Dennis Kimbro combines best-selling author Napolean Hilll's law of success with his own vast knowledge of business, contemporary affairs, and the vibrant culture of Black America to teach you the secrets to success used by scores of black Americans" - Dennis Kimbro

Steal Like An Artist: 10 Things Nobody Told You About Being Creative
by Austin Kleon

"You don't need to be a genius, you just need to be yourself. That's the message from Austin Kleon, a young writer and artist who knows that creativity is everywhere, creativity is for everyone. A manifesto for the digital age, Steal Like an Artist is a guide whose positive message, graphic look and illustrations, exercises, and examples will put readers directly in touch with their artistic side." - Austin Kleon

The Business of Expertise: How Entrepreneurial Experts Convert Insight to Impact + Wealth
by David C. Baker

"This passionate expertise manifesto is intended to elevate the impact of advisors who sell insight as entrepreneurs. Three foundational chapters form the basis of the entire book: experts develop insight by isolating patterns in data; they convert those insights to wealth by crafting a unique positioning for which few available substitutes exist; and their confidence grows as the marketplace embraces their application of expertise." - David C. Baker

Dedicated to the memory of Christopher Rockwell. Your friendship and loyalty has been unparalleled. Im grateful for having known you and your family.

Dedicated to the memory of Nipsey Hussle. Your music and words inspired me to reach my full potential. Im grateful to have lived when you walked this earth.

Thank You

To the most high for allowing me to use my talents for good
To my family, who has supported me throughout my career and business endeavors.
To my friends, who have always served as an extended family.
To my lovely HBCU Prairie View A&M University who helped shape me through life experiences.
To my Hometown Texarkana and Liberty Eylau ISD who help sparked my initial creativity.
To all the people that inspired me and took the time to give me information.

Planning Care for Children
in Respite Settings

Karina Has Down Syndrome
One Family's Account of the Early Years with a Child who has Special Needs
Cheryl Rogers and Gun Dolva
ISBN 1 85302 820 7

When I'm Away From Home
Jean Camis
ISBN 1 85302 898 3

Transition and Change in the Lives of People with Intellectual Disabilities
Edited by David May
ISBN 1 85302 863 0

The Child's World
Assessing Children in Need
Edited by Jan Horwath
ISBN 1 85302 957 2

User Involvement and Participation in Social Care
Research Informing Practice
Edited by Hazel Kemshall and Rosemary Littlechild
ISBN 1 85302 777 4

Planning Care for Children in Respite Settings
'Hello, This is Me'

Helen Laverty and Mary Reet

Jessica Kingsley Publishers
London and Philadelphia

First published in the United Kingdom in 2001 by
Jessica Kingsley Publishers Ltd
116 Pentonville Road,
London N1 9JB, England
and
325 Chestnut Street,
Philadelphia, PA 19106, USA.

Library of Congress Cataloging in Publication Data
Laverty, Helen, 1961-
Planning care for children in respite settings : hello this is me / Helen Laverty and Mary Reet
p. cm.
Includes bibliographical references and index.
ISBN 1-85302-936-X (pbk : alk paper)
1. Handicapped children--respite care. 2. Handicapped children--Respite care--Planning. I. Reet, Mary, 1960- II. Title.
HV888. L38 2001
362.1'989285889--dc21
2001029761

British Library Cataloguing in Publication Data
A CIP catalogue record for this book is available from the British Library

ISBN 1 84310 002 9

Printed and Bound in Great Britain by
Athenaeum Press, Gateshead, Tyne and Wear

For all those families.

This book is dedicated to Verity,
who will never be measured
by what she cannot do.

Acknowledgements

We would like to acknowledge the invaluable help of Caroline Smith and to thank her for her support, encouragement and common sense, and most of all for her commitment to the model in practice. Helen would like to thank Annie and John for living the model with her. Mary would like to thank Paul and her family for their support during a year when she found out for herself about having extra special needs.

Contents

Introduction

All children are special. All children have special needs but because of a physical, psychological, social or spiritual deficit some children have extra special needs. These children and their primary care givers are often left voiceless and consigned to the periphery of health and social care. This model aims to begin to redress that imbalance and contends that all children are special. By taking time to find out and then articulate how special each child is then their unique needs can be met.

The aim of *Planning Care for Children in Respite Settings* is to:

- promote independence for children who have special needs

- listen effectively to their parents

- reflect the concept of ordinariness for children who have special needs

- improve the lived experience of respite care for children who have special needs

- demonstrate effective partnerships in care.

Throughout the book the word 'respite' is taken to mean a gift of time for both children and their families that encompasses:

- therapeutic opportunity

- quality time

○ independence

○ the living of life, for all family members.

The book describes the search for and subsequent development of a brand new model to measure and promote independence, 'This is me', and an informal assessment schedule, 'Hello, this is me', which enhances that gift of time.

'Quality time' throughout the book is taken to represent time which appears to have no purpose but which reminds the carer and the child of the individuality and uniqueness of that child. The word 'parent' is used as an asexual term to describe the person or persons who have 24-hour responsibility for the child. 'Skilled adult carer' is used to cover a multidisciplinary group of personnel from both health and social care settings. 'The child' refers to that unique individual – the purpose of our care!

Children deserve to have a good quality of care no matter what their ability. *The Millennium Charter for Children's Health Services* (Action for Sick Children 1999, see Appendix 3) highlights several clear principles, which we have incorporated into this model and philosophy of care. One of the most important for us is Item 3, which talks about the empowerment of parents. In the government objectives for children's social services (Department of Health 1999) the first objective considers the importance of children being securely attached to family for the duration of childhood. One of the methods suggested is the provision of opportunity for parents to assist their child to be as successful as possible in developing independence.

Alderson (2000) when discussing children's rights says, 'A mentally or physically disabled child should enjoy a full and decent life, in conditions which ensure dignity, promote self-reliance and facilitate the child's active participation in the community' (p.46). 'This is me' and 'Hello, this is me' provide opportunities to promote this for children being cared for in a variety of settings in addition to their home environment.

Planning Care for Children in Respite Settings has been written with the aim of improving respite services for children, their families and the respite providers. We (the authors) believe it is long overdue. We want our book to be read, understood and implemented; therefore every attempt has been made to ensure the use of academic language is kept to a minimum. It is our intention that the reader will be captured by the philosophy we espouse and recognise that it is central to the promotion of independence and ordinariness.

The book opens with a chapter on family-centred care written by Mary Reet. The chapter addresses the principles of partnership in care from three perspectives: the parent, the skilled adult carer and the child. It provides an overview of the current theoretical standpoints on family-centred care, while offering a new perspective on the integration of ordinariness.

The second chapter of the book is a reflective account, written by Helen Laverty, of how and why the model was developed. It includes a schedule of four workshops to orientate a staff group to the model and philosophy of working. The chapter has as a basic tenet a commitment process for all who are involved in the child's care to take on board.

The next four chapters look at the practicalities of a systematic approach to reflecting ordinariness and promoting independence in a child's life. This part of the book contains reflective activities for the reader and is illustrated with case studies. It also includes anecdotal evidence from parents. This section of the book is written by Helen Laverty.

Chapter 7 looks at independence resulting from the utilisation of the model and its implementation across all spheres of a child's life, and reflects the beliefs of both the authors. Chapter 8, written by Mary Reet, provides the reader with an overview of government legislation that impacts on the accessing and delivery of respite care. Helen Laverty concludes the book with a chapter which examines the potential for this model to live and grow up with people who have extra special needs.

Appendices 1 and 2 contain photocopiable versions of, respectively, the tool for assessing children's care needs and the 'Hello, this is me' model. Appendix 3 sets out the provisions of *The Millennium Charter for Children's Health Services*.

The beliefs that formed the starting point for our deliberations follow.

- Individuals, regardless of their age, gender or label, should receive care that is based on their unique needs, that is appropriate in its design, and effective in its delivery.

- For children with a learning disability respite care is as ordinary as a sleepover with grandparents, it is an integral part of their lives; therefore a seamless web of services should be provided that ensures continuity and promotion of independence.

- No one knows a child better than the parents.

- If children with a learning disability are always described by what they cannot do, then a culture of 'never will do' could follow.

- Respite care needs to be planned and have purpose.

- Respite care is neither the long-term answer nor the solution to a problem.

- Planned care is a right.

Who do you see?

Who do you see when you walk through the door
When you've hung up your coat
Said 'hello' to the cat
Accepted a coffee
And heard me scream?

Who do you see when you enter my room?
After tapping the door (a rule to be obeyed)
And fixing your grin
And seen the mess
Who do you see?

Who do you see when you sit down for lunch?
And extolling the virtues
Start spooning the slop into my mouth
And I spit it back
Who do you see?

What do you see when I start to giggle
And my body twists up
And I snort and sniffle
Who do you see when I shout and I'm happy
With my arms waving and my legs thrashing
Who do you see?

Who do you know at the end of my visit?
When you've read my case notes
And listened to the care staff
And heard for yourself the row I can make?
And written a review?
And think that you can care for me?
Just ask yourself the question
But do you know me?

CHAPTER I

Family-Centred Care?

...at no time should any decision be taken about a handicapped child that would not be considered right for an ordinary child. And the age and the particular needs of each individual child should always take precedence over administrative convenience. (Oswin 1984, p.176)

Family-centred care is a tradition of child health nursing over the past 20–30 years. Key principles of family-centred care suggested by Pillitteri (1999, p.5) are:

The family is the basic unit of society.

Families represent racial, ethnic, cultural and socio-economic diversity.

Children grow both individually and as part of a family.

Folden and Coffman (1993) identify five main assumptions related to family-centred care:

1. Family is constant while service personnel change.

2. Collaboration is important at all stages of health care.

3. Policies and programmes should be comprehensive to include emotional and financial needs.

4. Family strengths and individual styles of coping should be respected.

5.   Health care should be flexible, accessible and respond to family needs.

Above all, family-centred care recognises the centrality of the family in the child's life and therefore their plan of care. It also acknowledges diversity in family structure and cultural identities (Ahmann 1994).

The philosophy espoused by many professionals is that children are cared for in consultation with their families and in an atmosphere of partnership. In reality some of the relationships which have developed with parents and carers cannot always be described as partnerships. Too often parents have been seen as a necessary part of the child's care but have been excluded from decision making or from making informed choices about the plan of care (Darbyshire 1994). This sounds harsh and is probably not intended but the idea that 'nurse knows best' disempowers parents who are often far more likely to know how to care for their child. There can be several reasons for this phenomenon. From a professional standpoint perhaps the carers feel somehow unable to ask parents how to care for their children as they feel the parents will expect a level of knowledge about basic childcare and will not have confidence in the carer's ability if they have to ask. Perhaps some carers lack communication skills to discuss care with parents in order to enable them to become true partners in care. Perhaps some junior members of staff (and maybe some senior ones as well) feel they have to appear as though they know everything (even if they do not). From the parent's perspective it may be that some parents do not want to be partners in care, they may have struggled for a long time and want someone to come in and 'take over'. The parents may feel that talking about partnership means signing up to learn to do complex medical tasks for their child even if they do not want to. Parents may also be reluctant as they may feel that they are being used as cheap labour to care for their child instead of an adequately staffed ward (Darbyshire 1994).

In respite settings parents are not expected to stay and participate in their child's care; however, in our view the development of effective partnership between home and respite is therefore essential. Parents need to know that the care their child is going to receive matches that which they would deliver. Acting in true partnership with parents can achieve this and this model acts as a tool to achieve this ideal in order to promote the care of children in the manner to which they are accustomed. Respect for parents and the work they do to promote their child's development and achievement of potential is important. Parents can receive numerous plans and programmes for their child. Cooper (1999, p.25) identifies three main indicators for good practice relating to family-centred care with families of children with chronic conditions. These are:

(a) to gain an understanding of the impact of those factors that influence a child and family's adaptation to chronic illness from the child and family's perspective

(b) to utilise this knowledge

(c) to negotiate strategies *with families* which enable the child to achieve growth and development potential [emphasis added].

Cooper (1999, p.14) also makes the point that the aim of care should be 'to provide support and care in order to promote as "normal" a family life as possible'. She emphasises the need to consider the impact of interventions on the child and family.

We believe that this model 'Hello, this is me' offers some control to parents to allow them to co-ordinate and manage their own child's care with a wide range of members from the multidisciplinary team. This should go some way to redress the balance and to emphasise the importance of seeing parents as equal partners in care.

In this chapter we want to look at family-centred care from a number of perspectives and hope to identify factors which contribute to successful family-centred care. The three main perspectives we shall use as a structure for discussion are the views of the parents, the carers and the child. All three perspectives offer some clarification about the successful features of family-centred care and the factors that can inhibit successful family-centred care. We have used some literature to expand on these views and offer alternative insights with the aim of providing an ideal view of how family-centred care should work at its most effective. In order for any kind of model of care to work family-centred care has to be understood and implemented.

The parents' perspective

An issue that is important when a child is cared for by a carer is the knowledge that the person chosen to care for the child will undertake the care in the same manner that the parent would. This principle affects all children, not just those with extra special needs, but is none the less important. The parent needs confidence that care will be carried out as they have asked. For example, a babysitter is looking after a group of children and the parent says that the bedtime is 7pm. The parent expects bedtime to be around that time. The reason that they give a time is to guide the babysitter about what is normal for the family. This prevents difficulties which may arise if, for example, the children do not go to bed until 9.30pm: they may have become over-excited and may not sleep soundly, they may have bad dreams or may have difficulty arising in the morning (particularly if it is a school morning). In fact the parent would probably not mind a little deviation, say to

7.30pm, but may be angry if their request appears to have been ignored, especially if they have to cope with the consequences of a tired child the next day!

Over the years of caring for their child parents become experts about their child (Millar 1994). They can be impatient with some carers who do not recognise the knowledge they hold (Pillitteri 1999).

Day (1997) points out the mixed feelings experienced by families who use respite services. He says that many parents feel insecure in approaching the carers who are looking after their child. Some parents may feel overawed in the presence of professionals and may feel unable to state what they want to happen because they feel that the 'nurse knows best'. One parent in a work by Brodin and Paulin (1997) expressed the view that their knowledge as the parent of a child with extra special needs was not accepted or endorsed by health care workers.

The difficulty arises when the parent wants to challenge decisions but feels overwhelmed by the professional. This is a feeling generated by the culture of respect that exists for nurses in society which inhibits questioning of their work. This is not always helpful as many nurses may not justify that respect. Parents can have difficulty putting their faith in carers they do not know (Flynn *et al.* 1995). This is why the establishment of trust is so important in building relationships between parents and carers. There has been a growing distrust of nurses and an increase in parents seeking more knowledge about their child's care over the past few years, with a number of high-profile cases about health professionals who abuse trust (Reet 1995). Parents are realising their possession of power to address the issue by questioning practice and asking for explanations (Millar 1994). This is something that all carers should encourage. It is not always an easy road to take for parents as they appear to question a higher authority, but it can yield results in better care for their child. As they appear to have a greater understanding of care issues then professionals will increasingly include them in the decision-making process (Robinson 1987).

Information is important in the empowering of parents (Gravelle 1997; Millar 1994). Finding out how systems work to gain services or support as well as knowledge about the child's illness can be important for parents in reducing unnecessary stress. Cooper (1999, p.106) states:

> Treatment for children with chronic illness is long term and if parents are to be enabled to care for their children then health professionals need to provide support that empowers them to make informed decisions within a framework that acknowledges them as equal partners in care.

Knafl *et al.* (1996) identify five family management styles when coping with children with chronic conditions. The five are on a continuum from Thriving through Accommodating, Enduring and Struggling to Floundering. When considering family styles of coping it perhaps should be remarked here that these might also be affected by cultural beliefs. The culture of the parents may regard disability as some form of punishment, which may cause the parents to feel a great deal of guilt and shame, in addition to any they might naturally feel (Alderman 1998).

Above all the most important aspect of family-centred care rests on communication between family and carers. In fact good communication is essential for the development of trust and the empowerment of parents which we have already discussed. Communication is the method by which information is imparted both from the professional to the parents and also from the parents to the professional. In work by Day (1997) five parents commented that communication between themselves and carers was an issue which was a disadvantage in respite care for them. They wanted to have some feedback on what their child had done while in the facility. Some suggested the use of a diary. One parent said: 'Sometimes it has been difficult to find out what she has been doing. Her own communication is at times difficult to understand if we do not know in general what she is talking about' (Day 1997, p.30).

The importance to parents of communication after a respite stay was highlighted in research by Oswin (1984). This information was necessary not just to reassure parents that the child settled and about what they did, but also to reassure the parents that their decision to use respite care was a good one. She identified that 'the degree of the parent's involvement in their children's care via personal contact with staff was crucial. It could make short-term care either a positive experience of sharing their children with other people or a negative experience of loss, lack of communication and strained relationships' (Oswin 1984, p.114). Oswin also found that notes kept about a child's stay were often medically orientated and did not convey any of their behaviour as children. What was noticeably lacking were notes on their emotional behaviour as children. She identified that better child-orientated records would make relationship forming more efficient. This again is something we feel that 'This is me' and 'Hello, this is me' seek to address.

Dick Sobsey (1999) talks about strategies that have helped him in parenting his child with extra special needs. He writes: 'Recognise that not all apparent support is helpful. Don't let anyone alienate you from your child. I needed support FOR my relationship with my child, not support away from him.' He also reminds us of the importance of seeing the positive contribution all children make to their family rather than looking at everything they cannot do. One of the recommendations from the work by Oswin (1984, p.197) is this: 'Any forms that parents are asked to fill in about their children should not only contain questions about their disabilities and weaknesses but also about their abilities and strengths.' Recognising and accentuating the positive is an important part of the philosophy of the model described in this book.

Many parents utilise the normalisation strategy, which is where usual family activities are maintained, focusing on the child's abilities and not on what is impossible to achieve (Cooper 1999). Parents also identify that contact with someone who understands what they have been through does help them to feel supported (Cooper 1999). Parents can feel that their personal difficulties are brushed aside when they encounter professional interventions (Pickard and Williams 1996). Day (1997) also found that parents of children with extra special needs may feel alienated by the services intended to help them. He also found that parents welcomed the chance to express their feelings and offer constructive criticisms. He emphasised that partnership is a living phenomenon that needs to be worked at and says, 'It cannot be assumed to exist simply because professionals are working with parents' (Day 1997, p.35). Over time, caring for a child with extra special needs, parents seem to become reconciled to the fact that most people are ignorant and socially inhibited (Pickard and Williams 1996), which is a sad indictment of society. Pickard and Williams also point out: 'Issues of shame, guilt and inadequacy make parents draw in on themselves and shun help, even when it is generously offered' (p.18).

Communication is part of the relationship-building process that enhances family-centred care in practice. The report *Don't Forget Us* (Mental Health Foundation 1997) talks about the need for a fine balance to be struck to achieve active partnership with parents and carers. It says:

Parents do not wish to be seen as a 'cheap resource' carrying out programmes for their child under the orders of professionals. But they do want to work in active partnerships with professionals, to be involved in decisions about their child's treatment and perhaps undertake some interventions themselves. In particular they want their views to be respected and given equal weight. (p.22)

Research by Brodin and Paulin (1997), which looked at respite care in Sweden, identified that many services do not ask parents what their needs are and do not evaluate the parents' views about whether the service fulfils those needs. Anecdotal evidence suggests that a similar situation exists in the UK, and is reflected in the case study material used in our book.

The carers' perspective

From a carer's perspective working in conjunction with parents can be threatening to their perceived knowledge or power. They may feel that they are the professionals so they should have all the answers in care matters. They may perceive themselves as the helping professional who helps this 'poor family' cope with this 'terrible problem'. The truth of the matter is that they are acting as substitutes for the parents so the parents can have some time which will in the end enable them to meet the needs of the child in their care for a much longer period. The image of children with extra special needs being a burden to their parents has led to a belief that they do not need the same consideration as ordinary children when going away from their families (Oswin 1984). Thus issues of homesickness of the children and the parent's grief at parting have not always been considered as they might have been for 'ordinary' children (Oswin 1984).

Carers may feel unable to own up to not knowing how to care for a child with a specific problem as they may feel they ought to know. They may not consider the idea that as the parent cares for this child most of the time the parent is the expert in caring for them (Millar 1994). This idea of the parent as expert is borne out in the work undertaken by Robinson (1987). She reports that parents expected acknowledgement of their knowledge by the professionals and a partnership approach. Instead many found themselves regarded with distrust by health professionals. However, if the parents' knowledge is taken advantage of this means the child will receive the care that most matches that which is 'delivered' at home. This meets the requirement that we maintain an environment which is as near as possible to the family's own when caring for the child in an alternative environment. Some research has indicated that although information is often collected by carers it is not always used in practice (Oswin 1984).

In work by Callery and Smith (1991) which considers the care of hospitalised children they remind us that the nurse is in a position of control over the relationship between nurses and parents:

> It is only the nurse who has the power to relinquish
> control and to choose to negotiate with the parents about
> roles or about care. If the nurse does not wish to negotiate
> the parent is not in a strong position to take the initiative.
> (p.776)

This can be translated into other care settings.

Oswin (1984) showed that carers can under-estimate the strength of love in existence between parents and their children with extra special needs. This can lead to differences in perception of the 'problems' the family face. There are difficulties with health professionals and parents having these differing perceptions of 'problems' and their solutions. Robinson (1987) reports of one parent's dissatisfaction when a medical solution to difficulty in eating, the insertion of a gastrostomy tube, was used. This intervention was seen as a success by the medical team but as a failure by the parents as they wanted to promote the child's oral intake. This short-term intervention by the medical team while meeting the child's short-term needs did not address his long-term prospects and possibly only increased his dependence on others. There needs to be careful consideration by carers about offering solutions, to make sure the nature of the difficulty or problem is fully understood. Perhaps some carers are afraid to ask parents, as they do not want to be told what to do. Perhaps some carers would rather make their own decisions about childcare than support parents in their preferred way. Perhaps some carers believe that 'nurse knows best'. Perhaps we should recall the words of Baines (2000, p.24), 'A bad nurse is like a bad mother – more into care and control than care and concern', in order to retain some healthy perspective about our role as a carer.

Wooley *et al.* (1989, p.117) looked at nurses working in a hospice situation and noted that 'staff valued having time to share with families and colleagues especially to enable them to respond to individual needs and to continue the child's preferred personal routine'. So it is also clear that some care providers are already making significant improvements and making time for adequate communication.

Whatever the answer the importance of clear communication is evident again and again. The management of parents' initial contact with the service is important in the building of relationships. In any patient-centred or family-centred situation communication is paramount, but more so with those who have extra special needs. The carer needs to balance professional behaviour with a recognition and respect for the patient as an individual human being (Baines 2000). Ahmann (1994) lists several features of a collaborative relationship as given by Bishop, Woll and Arango (1993) and Cross (1988). These features are communication, dialogue, active listening, awareness and acceptance of differences and negotiation. Another important part of the relationship between carers and parents is that of affirmation in order to encourage the parents in their coping (Whyte 1992). The parents need to be told that they are coping well and caring well for their child.

The child's perspective

Even if the child is able to participate in identifying what they want they are not always included in choices that can be made about their own care. With the full range of communication devices available it is only the severely challenged child who is going to find it difficult to offer a view about everything. But perhaps more effort needs to be made to include children in the choices that they can make, especially as children with extra special needs have the same feelings as ordinary children.

If care is not planned to follow what parents do there is the problem that care children receive is not always consistent. Consistency in care is an important aspect of a child's care that enables the child to make sound developmental growth. For example, imagine that one morning you are encouraged to put on your own clothes and struggle with the fastenings (although your mum has put fastenings on which you can manage with the minimum of effort). The next morning someone takes over your dressing routine and completely dresses you including the fastening with almost no help from you apart from co-operation. Is it any wonder that some children craving their independence fight with carers who try to do everything for them by removing their co-operation? It may be their only way of saying, 'I want to do this myself but if you won't let me I'll make it nearly impossible for you!' On a personal note I remember my sister who had a physical disability from birth, but who was determined to do everything for herself and would not allow anyone to help her. I remember the determination in her face and the anger if anyone helped (even if they meant well!).

Children in respite care can undergo 'normal' behavioural changes as a result of separation from their parents and home surroundings. This is not always recognised by either parents or carers as 'normal' separation anxiety (Oswin 1984). Perhaps the recognition of this likely reaction may promote good practice where these children are cared for by encouraging an attempt to ameliorate the separation anxiety by adequate preparation for respite commensurate with the child's individual personality. The keeping of the records of their stay can promote the link between respite and home. Consistency in care and the use of familiar items may also help (for example, an item the child holds for the parents as a sign that they are coming back).

Pillitteri (1999) reminds us that children with extra special needs may have difficulty in achieving autonomy or independence as a result of their developmental challenges. Encouraging children in the achievement of as much independence as possible is important to enhance their self-esteem as they grow towards adulthood. There is a danger with a child who has chronic problems that they may be over-protected so much that potential development is not achieved (Pillitteri 1999). For example, in a small study reported by Davies (1996) it is suggested that respite care provided by suitable skilled workers would increase social skills development in autistic children. However, Millar (1994) suggests that there is a fine line between allowing a child to develop at their normal rate and encouraging development in certain areas.

It may be that some children will use inconsistency in care to 'play up' staff. Perhaps to make out they are more disabled than they really are, or to pretend there are some things they are not allowed to do! Our argument is that where there is an ongoing model of care children will be known by their carers.

Any new staff or new people in contact with the child should be able to acquaint themselves with the child's ability from the beginning.

Communication remains important with this aspect of care and giving children the opportunity to be consulted about their care is vital. Children are individuals with unique needs and deserve the opportunity to express these whatever level of independence they achieve (Day 1997). They may not have control over a lot that happens but if choice can be given about what they can choose this promotes well-being. Minkes, Robinson and Weston (1994) suggest that many children are not consulted and have no control over their placements for respite care. Oswin (1984) notes that children can be disturbed if their respite care is planned in a secretive manner. Also, if children are not involved in making decisions about their own care they will be ill prepared for the transition to adult services, where more choice may be offered (Cooper 1999).

CHAPTER 2

'Hello, This is Me'

Why I began to formulate the model
(by Helen Laverty)

In 1998 I was approached by a charitable respite care home to provide help and support during a re-focusing exercise on the service offered to children with special needs and their families. The home, Rose Garth, provided reactive respite care to children and young people who all had varying degrees of learning disability. Rose Garth was deemed able to care for up to six children at any one time – with 97 children and their families being registered to access the service.

Rose Garth had been the original idea of a group of parents, and had fulfilled the immediate needs of families, but the following question needed to be asked: were the needs of the child in receipt of care being effectively met?

It was apparent, from the outside looking in, that the nature of the respite provided was for the benefit of the primary carers or family of origin, and all too often a period of respite was inappropriate because of the way children were grouped, or not grouped, as the case might be, together. An antiquated dependency rating was in place, which relied heavily on the child's presenting problem rather than their developing needs; this often provided the reasoning for grouping children together. As is often the case with an outside observer, simple strategies to begin to improve care were easily seen. I did not just wish to shore up the existing care, but was fired to improve and radically change the way respite was thought of by parents, delivered by skilled adult carers and lived as an experience by children who have a learning disability.

So where to start? An extensive literature search revealed little in the way of an appropriate model that would describe children by what they could do, meet the service requirements of the environment and match the skills mix of the staff team. Once I had agreed to help, I needed to set myself some aims and objectives, as well as articulating the philosophy that underpinned the care I wished to see delivered. This proved to be the catalyst for change and the springboard for success.

In this chapter I will describe the process I went through to find and implement a suitable model to match the re-focused philosophy. It is important at this stage to acknowledge the part played by the staff from Rose Garth, the children who accessed respite and their parents in enabling me to be successful in describing 'Hello, this is me'.

Once a commitment had been made to change the focus of the way care was offered, provided and implemented then a model that matched the 're-think' was next on my agenda. With a new philosophy in place it was important that the care delivery system matched the commitment to promote independence.

'This is me' was written to provide a picture of the individual child's changing needs, while also providing a logical developmental process through which the child's changing needs could be measured. Each aspect of the independency criteria equates to a points system, which in turn gives the child an extra special care score that determines the amount of staff support that child requires. The independency criteria consist of ten headings, which were influenced by the activities of living model of nursing (Roper, Logan and Tierney 1983) and the concept of 'ordinariness' as reflected by O'Brien's service accomplishments (1987).

- Rest, sleep and night-time care

- Personal care

- Breathing

- Communication

- Emotional, spiritual and cultural needs

- Playing and learning

- Personhood (what I know about me)

- Maintaining safety

- Eating and drinking

- Out and about.

Each criterion is broken down into descriptions of 'ordinary factors' that impact on that aspect of the uniqueness of each child, ranging from an ordinary completion of the task to the out of the ordinary (see Appendix 1). For example, 'Rest, sleep and night-time care' includes descriptions/indicators of a range of factors that go towards describing what is ordinary for that child to ensure an independent individualised amount of sleep each night.

The next task was to place a notional value on each activity, thus providing some framework from which the plan to meet care needs and promote independence could be drawn. To arrive at a time value to equate to 1 a sample set of parents of children with and without disabilities, ranging in age from 18 months to 15 years, were asked, 'On an ordinary day, how long would it take you and your child to complete this activity?' (Selected from a menu of everyday activities.) From this a general consensus was reached that 15 minutes was an adequate amount of time to spend on an ordinary activity on an ordinary day. This then provided an independence description for groups of children.

- 30–40 care delivery points (high level of emerging independence)

  This child has an ordinary routine that needs the support of a specialised adult carer to promote the development of further independence.

- 41–60 care delivery points (moderately independent)

  This child needs prompts and supports from a specialised adult carer. S/he needs a holistic structured environment to provide opportunity for independence.

- 61–100 care delivery points (low level of independence)

  This child has extra special needs, which require a specialised adult carer to promote his/her personhood.

- Over 100 care delivery points (dependent on others)

  This child requires the one-to-one support of a skilled adult carer to facilitate his/her life skills.

The Roper et al. model (1983) has as a basic care premise that people are engaged in the process of living, and that this process can be broken down into 12 activities, in which an individual moves through a continuum from 'totally dependent' to 'independent' throughout their life cycle. In the Roper et al. model the belief is stated that an individual's personality is reflected in their own individualised performance of the activities of living.

It was my premise that if children who have a learning disability are always described by what they cannot do then not only can a culture of 'never can do' follow, but also the children may never be viewed in a positive light, and provided with opportunity from which to springboard to success. It was important to reflect the fact that parents and families often have a realistic view of their child. Also, the individual disability was viewed as being ordinary rather than out of the ordinary and was seen as just another facet of the individual child's personality.

So how does this translate into care delivery time?

Once the child has been accurately described, and an independence rating arrived at, then this can be used to plan care and group children of similar abilities together. To implement the model effectively a re-think of how services were organised, offered and delivered needed to come about.

At the outset respite was offered on a combination of either ad hoc, planned or 'first come first served' basis. As with most care establishments a minimum staffing to children ratio was employed. This meant that children of mixed ages and more importantly mixed abilities were banded together in a care situation that had neither the resources nor the underpinning parameters to do anything other than foster dependency.

'This is me' sets about to challenge this concept, and alter the practice, by:

1.   ensuring that the maximum amount of staffing support required to promote independence is offered to each child during his/her stay in respite

2.   planning respite for each child who accesses the service on a regular basis with children of similar ages,

interests and independence, thus ensuring respite has purpose and benefit for the child

3.   matching the total care needs of any one group of children to the number of staff rostered to be on duty.

Most models of resource management rely on a concept that supplies the minimum number of staff to support a prescribed number of children. It was important that we remained aware of the need to ensure the new model was cost-effective and promoted optimum independence for all the children who accessed the service. Therefore the model was piloted on the premise that each member of staff has their rostered hours of duty broken down into 'care delivery bites' (i.e. the number of 15-minute segments available in their working day). For example, a care assistant who is employed on a full-time basis will work a day-time shift of 7.5 hours. When breaks are deducted (30 minutes) this equates to a start point of 28 care delivery bites. This figure then needs multiplying by the number of children each care assistant is designated to care for in the care philosophy of each home, for example, three, and we then arrive at a care delivery bite score of 84. This number is added to the total staff score for the rostered shift, and then an accurate interpretation will be arrived at of how many children can be cared for and have their independence promoted on any one shift, by dividing the individual child's care points into the total staff complement of care bites for that shift.

A typical shift

One care delivery bite = approximately 15 minutes

Each care assistant works a shift of 7.5 hours. When breaks are deducted that equates to 28 care delivery bites. The minimum staff ratio is one care assistant to three children.

Therefore, if a care assistant has 28 bites per child, they have a rating of 84 care delivery bites.

Senior care staff work shifts of 7.5 hours. When breaks and 60 minutes for administration/managerial activities are deducted that leaves 24 care delivery bites. If each senior care staff member cares for two children per shift that gives each senior care staff member 48 care delivery bites.

On a typical shift, with one senior care staff and four care assistants, this would mean that a group of children whose total independency rating added up to no more than 384 could be cared for.

The implementation has not been without its pitfalls. For example, the staff were used to having a prescribed number of children at any one time, and a minimum number of staff to care for them. With the implementation of 'This is me' there are often shifts where there are more staff than children, but those children present with such complex disabilities that it does take more than one carer to promote independence adequately for that child. Some shifts previously were always considered 'heavy' or 'difficult', because of the multiple physical impairments some children presented with. Staff now appreciate that with an accurate description of independence the right number of staff will be on duty to care for that child.

Parents have had to re-think why they use respite, and who derives the most benefit from it. Managers have needed to consider the minimum staff to children ratios and whose needs they best served.

As models of care reflect personal philosophies about concepts such as ordinariness, personhood and, for example, 'living a life' as opposed to 'being alive', we do not envisage that 'This is me' will stay static, and we invite the reader to evolve the model with its basic philosophy intact to promote independence for the groups of children with whom they work.

The next step

Once the rating scale was in place the whole care planning documentation needed to be reviewed. It was important to reinforce and reflect the underpinning philosophy that parents know their children best. A family-friendly approach was called for to enable parents to pass on accurately a description of their own child's care needs. 'Hello, this is me' sets out to start the partnership between families and care givers to provide that seamless web of care the children deserve.

It is envisaged that the care planning document is a 'living entity' that follows the child from home to school to respite, thus providing an accurate record of what is now happening and what has happened in the child's life so far. Obviously accurate recordkeeping is a necessity in any care establishment and an element of duplication will occur, but as the package is easily set up on disk a paper copy can follow each child.

The headings for 'Hello, this is me' are not scientifically rooted, but come from what I need care givers to know about my child before I am happy to leave her (see Appendix 2).

The documentation was piloted amongst parents who use Rose Garth. From a personal perspective the first mother I worked with had a profound effect on the rest of the way the system has developed. I visited this lady at home, and explained the paperwork to her, and why it was necessary to re-focus the way Rose Garth operated. After some initial hesitation she agreed to talk to a total stranger about her son's habits and foibles. The meeting lasted two hours and at the end of it I felt I knew this young man well, and would be confident to begin to care for him. His mother thanked me for 'wanting to know about him' and was excited about being part of the project. She added useful suggestions to the format and confided that it was the first time in 14 years that anyone had asked about the ordinariness of her son's life: 'People usually only want to know about how wrong things are going, the out of the ordinary, not the ordinary, the things that make us a family and "Jamie" a person.'

From this meeting Jamie's mother and I were able to write a care plan to ensure that a consistent approach is used to work with Jamie and his inappropriate expression of his own sexuality. The language used, while being explicit, was language his mother and father were comfortable with, but also left the implementers (school and respite) with no ambiguity. The care plan not only aimed to provide a consistent approach in this young man's life, but also empowered his family.

Moving forward

I now had a working copy of the model, a care plan of a child that the care staff knew well, and ideas relating to measuring independence; all I had to do was sell the package to the senior staff team!

It could be argued that their support should have been secured from the beginning. Personally this caused me some anxiety, as it is not my style to work in isolation, but the staff were aware that I was undertaking some sort of project work with the manager and that her mission was change, so maybe it did not come as too much of a surprise.

I agreed to facilitate four workshops that would bring the senior staff on line.

Workshop 1

Why bother care planning?

AIM

To provide all senior staff with the opportunity to explore the concept of care planning within the work environment.

OBJECTIVES

By the end of the day the participants will have had the opportunity to discuss:

1. what care planning entails

2. the current position in the home on care planning

3. the need for change

4. the way forward.

Initially the staff were very hostile, and the majority of the first hour was spent rapport building with them. The tool that provided the most leverage in effecting change was the completed documentation that I had on Jamie's life, and his needs. For the care staff the description of his independence seen through the eyes of his mother was a revelation. Little things were highlighted as care needs which were not being met, not through carelessness, but because care staff had become used to delivering care to the presenting issue rather than planning a service to promote independence. The team had lost sight of Jamie as he grew up and began to express all the facets of himself, particularly his sexuality, through inappropriate channels. No one had looked further than the end of his or her nose to ask why or to plan how. More importantly no one (at home, respite or school) had shared their strategy or articulated what was acceptable/unacceptable behaviour in their opinion. The potential for extra negative labels to be attached to this young man was tremendous and frightening as a

The first request for respite
A cute preschool child is having problems at night

Respite begins

Child starts school
Sleeps much better

Respite continues

Family go abroad on holiday

Respite increases

Child's behaviour deteriorates
Travel arrangements to and from home altered
Staff reluctant to take him out
Medication review requested
Excluded from school trip due to inappropriate behaviour

Has anyone asked what the behaviour is?

**Haven't we lost sight of whom we were providing
respite for and why?**

Think of a child you care for.
Regularly?
Do you know why they receive respite?
Are you sure?

Figure 2.1 Losing sight of why a child receives respite

reflective exercise for care providers. Eventually, using the knowledge I had gained from talking to Jamie's mother, it was relatively easy to make the transition to planning care effectively.

By the end of the day, an element of team cohesiveness had entered into the proceedings (I had never considered how isolated they felt from each other); the team were ready to run with the care planning documentation.

Workshop 2

Commitment!

All people involved in the child's care have to be committed to the process of care planning and its aims to promote and develop the child's independence.

For care planning to be successful, you have to display an attitude to the child and his family that allows you to build a relationship, based on mutual trust and respect. The child and his family need to be sure that you are genuine in your intentions, knowledgeable, reliable and friendly.

The child needs to know that you respect him, and are an integrated part of his care.

The child's family need to know that you recognise their child's potential, worth and uniqueness, and are partners with them in the independence process.

The components of care planning

This workshop required the whole philosophy of care planning to be explored with the senior care team and, perhaps more importantly, their role in the care planning process to be discussed. Before this began we needed a statement of commitment to both the children and the need for change.

This commitment process was influenced for me by the work of Ashworth (1980) and her aims of nursing, but also by a personal belief that care for people who have a learning disability is about life skill facilitation.

Workshop 3
The new documentation

The aim of this workshop was to give staff the opportunity to get a feel for the paperwork, before they actually went out and worked with it. Again, completed assessment documentation of real children was used alongside fictitious case study material. The senior care team were given opportunity to analyse the process critically and offer suggestions, while learning to plan care in a safe environment. The main issue that was highlighted was the 'skewed' picture of need the night-time rating gave, and the need to extract that figure in terms of independence and staff support from the 24-hour continuum (see Chapter 7 and Appendix 1).

Workshop 4
Implementation

It was agreed at Workshop 3 that each member of the senior care team was to be allocated four children, with whom they would undertake the care planning process, and that the fourth workshop would be dedicated entirely to reflection on that process. A deadline of six weeks was set and armed with the papers we sent the team out. The response was variable, but in providing a supportive environment in which the staff were able to reflect, shortcomings were identified in individuals' interactional abilities. Never before had the team needed to communicate so much with mothers and fathers! Further staff training and support were offered to the team in order to develop these skills in them.

So where are we now?

All the children who use Rose Garth now have a care plan that is agreed by their parents; respite is planned to ensure the child has opportunity to meet the maximum independence with staff support; and all newly referred children have an independence rating undertaken before the first planned admission (emergencies will always be an exception). Care is more proactive, and parents and carers actually talk to each other about what has happened to a child!

CHAPTER 3

Assessment
The Key to Accurate Care Planning

> Individuals receive care that is based on their unique needs. (Laverty and Reet 2000, p.2090)

Ineffective assessment leads to ineffective care that is service-led, and has little person focus. 'Hello, this is me' is not intended to replace any scientific tool, but is designed to enhance the ordinariness of the child's life, and enhance the concept of personhood through all care environments. The intention is to promote a sense of continuity that builds on independence and reinforces individuality.

The 1989 Children Act states 'that accommodation for children with disabilities should not be unsuitable for their needs' (HMSO 1989, Vol.6, p.30) and that 'respite care should be provided in the context of a package of care for families' (p.32). The act goes on to identify seven criteria that support 'a more appropriate flexible short-term care':

- A local service, where the child can continue to attend school as if still living at home.

- Good quality childcare in which parents have confidence and which ensures that the child is treated as a child first and then for any disability which may require special provision.

○ Planned availability. Research into different models of respite care has clearly indicated the importance of parents (and older children) choosing patterns of use and being able to use the service flexibly.

○ A service which meets the needs of all children. Concern has been expressed about the lack of respite for children with complex needs. The service should be available to children living with long-term foster carers or adoptive parents.

○ Care which is compatible with the child's family background and culture, racial origin, religious persuasion and language.

○ Age-appropriate care – so that young children and adolescents are given relevant care and occupation.

○ An integrated programme of family support which sees planned respite care as part of a wider range of professional support services to meet family needs. Escalating use of respite care may indicate a need for other family support services.

It has long since been recognised that children with a learning disability should not receive respite care in a long-stay or hospital environment. If we set about assessing the impact of respite not only on a child's life, but also on their whole family make-up, it is important that not only the bricks and mortar of the accommodation are considered. The purpose and philosophy that underpins the care is more important. 'Hello, this is me' not only supports this notion, but also reinforces it by ensuring that care planners, providers and deliverers reflect the ordinariness of each child in all aspects of the service, by this we mean that they utilise the assessment schedule both appropriately and effectively which promotes

- ○ partnership

- ○ equality

- ○ independence

- ○ opportunity to be ordinary

- ○ measurable success.

By taking the seven criteria of the 1989 Children Act as a bench mark for quality standards in conjunction with 'Hello, this is me', and acknowledging shortfalls in the current provision, we are moving children with a learning disability and their families away from the periphery of health and social care and brokering a much more integrated service that promotes equality of access in a mixed economy of care.

Case study

Rebecca Westbury

Rebecca is the only child of Dave and Claire Westbury; she is eight years old; she has a severe learning disability due to pre-maturity. Rebecca is pre-verbal, and unable to walk; she needs full assistance in everyday living skills to promote any sense of independence. Rebecca attends a local special school, which requires a 20-mile trip each way; she is picked up by taxi each morning at 7.45am and returns home at 4.45pm. Rebecca's parents run their own business, which is a small market garden, supplying organic vegetables to local cafés and bistros.

Rebecca receives respite care on Thursday and Friday nights throughout term time; her parents always collect her just before lunch on a Saturday. During the long summer holiday Rebecca has a planned two-week stay.

The home is finding Rebecca a difficult child to care for. The general opinion is that she is spoilt at home. Rebecca is difficult to feed, and has noisy restless nights, so much so that she is usually downstairs in the playroom for the majority of the night.

Rebecca's mother is aware that she does not like respite, but the family business cannot survive without Rebecca's absence each week. She does not find Rebecca difficult to feed, especially as she has found out how to thicken her foods and drink, using biscuits for sweet foodstuffs, white bread for savouries (no one has ever suggested thickeners to her). At home Rebecca sleeps for about ten hours; she always goes to bed at 7.30pm, and is turned at midnight and at 3am. (The Westburys were not asked about set times for turning Rebecca and they did not think to mention it.)

Rebecca has a severe visual impairment, for which glasses have been prescribed; she has a pair which are left at school, and a pair which are kept at home. Mrs Westbury does not send any to respite in case they get lost.

Rebecca loves to be outside, whatever the weather. The family dog, Tin-Tin, is her devoted companion; her mother and father have a lean-to porch next to their main growing area where Rebecca and Tin-Tin spend time, and it is brightly painted and adorned with wind chimes and mobiles to provide the maximum visual stimulation. Rebecca loves to listen to talking books if she cannot be outside, *Peter Rabbit* being her favourite.

Rebecca is well cared for at home, but at respite she has been given a collection of negative labels, the reason for her admission has been forgotten and the developing person lost sight of.

Activity

Spend a few minutes reflecting on the uniqueness of your life: the way you choose a meal, have your hair washed, spend undirected time.

Now think again about tasks and activities you do not / would not value in your life.

If you were unable to express your preference who would be able to pass on this information accurately for you?

Think of the admission procedures you have been involved in — would they elicit the necessary information for someone who does not know you to meet your needs holistically?

The process of assessment can appear complicated and, due to the focus of the assessment, it often leads to inappropriate decisions which in turn compound the negative labelling of the child.

It is important that all who are involved in the assessment of a child with extra special needs are clear about three things:

1. The purpose of the assessment – this may be to measure a child's strengths, identify a child's shortfalls, match a child to a service, or plan a programme to promote independence.

2. The need to share the assessment data with others involved in the child's care – this includes parents and/or primary carers; it is important that those in charge of the care services offered to any child with a disability are open and honest in their intentions. This means explaining to parents why decisions have been made; maybe the difficulties a service has with a child could be resolved if they were discussed with family. Perhaps the biggest challenge to the care services is that of explaining the aims of the care a child receives.

3. Assessment is not about secrets – from this follows a culture of openness built on mutual trust and respect, not only of each other, but of the individual child and the common goal.

For children who have a disability and their families, the way they live their lives is ordinary to them. Once that child moves to a respite care environment the way they live with their disability becomes 'out of the ordinary', and compounds feelings of difference, which in turn impacts on the way they are perceived in the care setting.

By working with families to describe what is ordinary for their child in the way they live their life and then incorporating this into the holistic care plan that is unique for each child, care providers are facilitating the maintenance and acquisition of life skills while the child is away from home.

Maureen Oswin in 1978 highlighted that children who live in long-stay hospitals can expect to receive an average of five minutes' mothering attention every ten hours. Writing again in 1984, she suggested that 'short-term care is a very dubious service, which had never been thought through in terms of good practices in childcare. It is often considered the answer to all family problems, but in reality, it may be creating more problems' (p.92).

Children deserve better. Parents need to be reassured that their child is receiving gold standard care while away from home and also that they are the directors of their child's care, the respite staff the enhancers. Utilising the concept of 'what is ordinary' in the assessment process means that while the child's development is not held static a label of developmental delay is reinforced; parents are afforded the opportunity of being partners in that developmental process, rather than being seen as the 'ones who can't cope'; we are then well on the way to ensuring children receive unique, effective and appropriate care.

A letter came from the team office, about my request for respite. From what I could understand, during the school year we were entitled to 15 days. (Was that overnight care? I wasn't sure.) We had wanted him to go to the Briar Patch, it's near to school, several other families we know use it, and it has an excellent reputation, but we had been placed on the list for Beach House. I had to look the address up on the local street map, the school journey alone would take 45 minutes, if there were no other pick-ups, and one of Damien's flash points is the bus… So I rang the team office to ask, 'Why?'

'Your son has a severe learning disability and his behaviour is challenging,' she said.

I thought: tell me something I don't know!

'Beach House is much better able to deal with Damien's behaviour and disabilities.'

But what about his needs and lifestyle, I wanted to know, how are we going to manage that bus journey?

'You must ring and make an appointment to see them,' she said and gave me the number.

As professionals we are all too aware of the need for accurate scientific assessment that provides the base line from which we can plan our interventions – but how important is it to parents? And, perhaps more importantly, how far does it go to instil confidence in the service for parents and ensure children receive gold standard care while in respite? Parents need to be reassured that the care their child receives dovetails that at home and that goals and priorities are shared between them and the respite provider.

Good communication – The key to effective partnership?

Any organisation that decides to utilise the 'Hello, this is me' approach will need first to undertake an audit of the communication skills of the staff involved in the assessment process. It is important to remember that we are asking parents and other primary carers to share ordinary but often intimate information about their child and what makes them a family. Also some parents and primary carers will need to be convinced of the relevance of the information you are asking for, and may never have considered their child's life in such minute and positive terms. By acknowledging the uniqueness of that individual child, professional care providers are identifying the need for effective and appropriate care. Taking that one step further the need for respite both for the child and the family of origin needs valuing in terms of its benefit and efficacy. Link all this to the philosophy underpinning the assessment schedule and it is imperative that we begin to assess the impact of the respite a child and family are already receiving. We then have a moral and professional obligation to be honest in our intentions and proactive in our delivery. We need to acknowledge that the professionals' perceptions of what a child cannot do has often been influenced by the design of the assessment schedule and translated into jargon and the myth of 'never will do'. Parents often have a more realistic view of their child; after all they are with them 24 hours a day, seven days a week.

Is this assessment schedule more than an admission checklist?

So we rang and made an appointment. The first two they offered us didn't give any opportunity for all of us to go as a family.

The man on the end of the phone said he'd catch up with Damien at school (huh!) so he needn't come – and was it really relevant for Claire and Carmel?

Having a learning disability, and living with that disability, is ordinary for that person and therefore that family. As professionals we often make assumptions about the make-up of individual families; those assumptions are often underpinned with a theoretical basis, and spurred on by a desire to control rather than identify the phenomena that make that family unique. By recognising the power of families and the importance they have in the ordinariness of life we are promoting harmony both at home and in respite.

Robina Shah describes the uniqueness of being born with a disability into an Asian family; what she writes in relation to the parental response to the label transcends cultural barriers and supports the importance of families.

> Disability, whether it is physical, mental, sensory or auditory, is not prejudiced in any way: it transcends all races, beliefs and cultures. It creates similarly profound emotional, practical and psychological experiences for all parents, whoever they are. Unfortunately, where Asian families are concerned, common sense about a valid generalisation of attitudes towards disability is lost in the mists of ignorance and perceived cultural differences. Little or no attention is given to what is in fact a natural and universal response to having a child who is born with a disability or who, later on in childhood, is diagnosed as disabled. Looking for differences where none exist or assuming homogeneity of feelings when differences need to be identified is a form of cultural racism. (Shah 1992, p.21)

Getting started

It is never easy to convince either a staff group or a consumer group (i.e. parents) that change must come about, particularly as 'Hello, this is me' gets you to ask questions about the lives of children you are supposed to know well.

Activity

Reflect on Rebecca's case history. Maybe share your thoughts with a colleague, or care partner. Look at the potential for negative labelling on the part of both her parents and the staff team. Ask yourself: where is Rebecca as a person reflected in her holistic package of care?

Asking questions

It is our experience that the best responses to the questions come when they are asked at home; primarily the family control the power base, and you are a guest in their home. By involving the whole family in describing what is ordinary for their child, brother, sister, or grandchild, you are acknowledging that they have a life, and a family life, you are also showing your interest in their child and commitment to planning in partnership.

Activity

At the back of this book is a copy of the assessment schedule (Appendix 1). Fill it in for your child, or a child you care for regularly. Now the test: is there any information that you as a parent have not thought important enough to pass on to the respite environment? Or for those of you who are paid carers, how many blanks are there in the life of a child you care for regularly?

In the end we couldn't let him go, I know I know maybe I'm over protective, but I just wasn't easy about the whole thing. We all talked about it as a family. Carmel, she's 14, was really worried what would happen if Damien kicked off.

'Has anybody asked us, Mum, what makes him blow, or even the best way to settle him?'

No one had. His dad's a bit more of a thinker than me, he wanted to know what the arrangements were if Damien just didn't settle and needed to come home.

'That won't happen,' we were told. Too right it won't, I'm looking into alternative arrangements. A lad in Damien's class is fostered twice a month on a share the care scheme – this has got to be a better option for us.

In 1999 the government published its objectives for children's social services. The summary identifies 11 objectives (Department of Health 1999):

- ensuring stable, secure and effective care for all children

- protecting children from abuse and neglect

- better life chances for children in need: good education, health care and social care for all children

- good life chances for children in care: good education, health care and social care

- enabling young people leaving care to live successful adult lives

- meeting the needs of disabled children and their families

- better assessment leading to better services

- actively involving users and carers

- using regulation to protect children

- making sure that child care workers are fit for the job

   ◦ making best use of resources: choice, effectiveness and value for money.

Join this with *The Millennium Charter for Children's Health Services* (Action for Sick Children 1999) (see Appendix 3), and a care package that reflects the uniqueness of a child's life, and gold standards for respite care are well within our grasp.

Case study

Melissa-Jayne McGinty

Melissa-Jayne is 18. She has a severe learning disability and displays severe challenging behaviours associated with an autism spectrum disorder. Currently she is a Monday-to-Friday boarder in a specialist school 25 miles from home. Melissa-Jayne is a challenge to those who care for her. She resists any attempt at physical contact, and will bite if she has a mind to. This has been particularly difficult for her family. She is the youngest of nine brothers and sisters, all of whom live within a five-mile radius of the parental home. Mr McGinty has angina, and it is believed that the stress of Melissa-Jayne living back at home full time will prove detrimental to his health. Mrs McGinty sees Melissa-Jayne as a special gift from God; she has always been unhappy with the idea of Melissa-Jayne living away from home. Corrine, who is the eldest daughter, is keen for Melissa-Jayne to live in a local residential facility. Funding is not a problem, neither is securing a place; the only problem is that Mrs McGinty believes that nobody can look after her daughter as well as her family can.

Activity

By engaging in dialogue, and building an effective rapport with Mrs McGinty, Melissa-Jayne and the rest of the family, 'Hello, this is me' could be used effectively to aid the transition from children's to adult services. Reflect on your own experiences and identify young people you have cared for and/or known. What information has been passed from one service to another, promoting continuity, maintaining independence and effectively planning for the future?

CHAPTER 4

Planning

Planned care does not detract from spontaneity. Planned care ensures that respite has purpose. If the reason for admission to respite is to enable the family to get some rest as the child does not sleep, we need to know why the child doesn't sleep and plan her care effectively to ensure an acceptable sleep pattern in developed; after all, sleep is the right of the child also. Planned care should be a human right.

Case study

Ray Livingston

Ray is 14 years old, and has a moderate learning disability, the aetiology of which is unknown. Over the past four years Ray has gained mastery over many of his independent living skills, and has been considered for a transfer to the local comprehensive school. His parents are resistant of such a move; particularly as of late Ray has been displaying inappropriate sexual behaviour. Over the last six months their requests for respite have increased to every other weekend and all half-term breaks, and a request has been received for four weeks during the summer break. Ray has twin sisters who are 11 years old and while the girls are described as loving Ray, it has been noted of late that Ray's behaviour curtails their own development, for example neither of them asks friends home, and both choose not to go on family outings if Ray is part of the equation.

Ray is described at school as being very independent, and is given an amount of responsibility. At home his environment is restricted, as is his ability to integrate with the community, because of his 'fixation' with sexually explicit talk and questions.

Activity

Spend some time considering the support you received as a young person in developing your own awareness of who you are, in other words the concept of personhood (O'Brien 1987). Now think again and apply those principles to your own child, or a young person whose care you are involved in. Do we ever give young people with learning disabilities the opportunity to grow up and use adult problem-solving strategies to promote their awareness of self?

In the 1998 NHS Executive document *Signposts for Success* Section 5 clearly sets out the principles of 'Good practice in specialist health services for people with learning disabilities'. Items 5.1–5.5 relate specifically to services for children and their families:

5.1 Skilled counselling, advice and support should be available to families at the time of diagnosis and subsequently. This involves both emotional and practical support.

5.2 It is essential that children with learning disabilities are regarded as children first and that their emotional and physical needs are recognised as well as those of the rest of the family.

5.3 There should be respite services, and services providing long-term care outside the home, that are able to meet the needs of those children with physical or mental health problems. Health services should work closely with local authority services to develop care packages for children with complex or severe health problems and disabilities.

5.4 Health service commissioners and providers are expected to contribute to the assessment of special educational needs (Education Act 1993) and have specific duties under the Children Act (1989). The Disabled Person's Act (1986) addresses some of the problems encountered by young disabled people moving into adult life.

5.5 There should be access to mental health services (including those for challenging behaviours and forensic services) that can offer early and effective intervention by staff with skills in working with children and adolescents with learning disabilities and emotional and behavioural problems.

It is time that services for children who have a learning disability recognised that children are children regardless of whatever other label has been attached to them. All human beings grow and develop physically, psychologically and socially – and templates that are laid down for the rest of the population (see for example Bowlby 1952; Erikson 1950; Piaget 1932; Vygotsky 1978) apply equally to children who have a learning disability; however, it is often the disability that is seen as the root of all issues rather than a developmental phase. It is important for us to acknowledge that children with a learning disability do grow up and, while their expectations and aspirations (alongside those society have for them) can be altered due to their disability, in essence issues such as the following do impact on the child who has a learning disability:

- ° attachment and separation (Bowlby 1953)

- ° industry versus inferiority developmental phase (Erikson 1950)

- ° initiative versus guilt developmental phase (Erikson 1950)

- ° identity versus role confusion developmental phase. (Erikson 1950)

By acknowledging who they are, and identifying their developmental needs rather than reinforcing the negative label of developmental delay, a more holistic picture is drawn of the child and it follows that life skill acquisition is a real opportunity.

Planning is an integral part of life; it contributes to our sense of well-being, mastery and self-actualisation; the need to recognise partnership in planning in an individual's life is long overdue.

It was time for Isabel's annual review. It's funny really – most of my friends couldn't wait to get their kids' school reports. I'd listened to how many 'A's Sammy had got, and how the school wanted Kim to try out for the county swimming trials, Joy had even moaned about how little her Lizzie's teacher really knew about her. I'd watched them buy treats as rewards and plan end-of-term barbeques. Well, now it was our turn, I wondered how many 'A's Isabel could get. If they gave them out for 'fitting' in the supermarket we'd win hands down. Anyway, there we sat, me, Dave the community nurse, Mrs Swift her class teacher and some young girl from respite who introduced herself as Isabel's associate worker (now what does that mean?).

Dave talked about her latest medication review, and how her seizures were now under control. (Is that worth an 'A'?)

Mrs Swift talked about her improved concentration (definitely a star in my book).

Caitlin (the associate worker) talked about the difficulties they had with Isabel, how she cries a lot, and is aloof from the other children.

Then they talked about what their plans were for my daughter next year: increased horse riding, a Makaton symbol board, continuing with the respite arrangements.

'Hang on a minute,' I thought, 'she's nearly 14, isn't this her options year?'

Activity

Think about your own life in terms of milestones: the things you have achieved and are really proud of. Maybe narrow it down to a specific chronological period, follow them through in logical sequence, and use symbols to represent choice, life enhancers, gate keepers and traffic lights (i.e. obstacles and blockages) that were put in your way (see Figure 4.1).

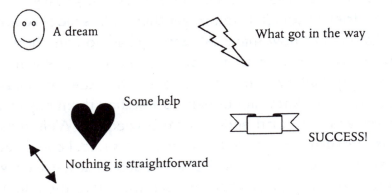

Figure 4.1 Examples of symbols

Now think about your role in the life of a child who has a learning disability. How often has your role been less than positive in providing both support and opportunities? Think about care plans in which you have had an active role – whose life did they really benefit?

I was beginning to think that no one had anything really good to say about our girl. I was glad of the extra horse riding, and the Makaton symbols, and I wouldn't have minded some home care support. Then Caitlin pipes up:

'It is our opinion that Isabel needs an increased identity, particularly within her peer group. We'd like to suggest a change in her respite service.'

'Here we go!' I thought. Anyway, what she wanted to do was change the nights each month Isabel stays away from home so that she can be with a group of girls her own age, and go to youth club at the local church hall. Let's be serious, she's got a severe learning disability! She wears nappies, she has fits – what good is make-up and Boyzone to her?

The process of planning involves reviewing all the variables and 'stepping' a course of action to achieve a desired outcome.

All too often children who have a learning disability are described by what they cannot do rather than by what they can do. As professionals it is important to be honest in our intentions, this includes acknowledging that the myth of 'can't do' is often influenced by the design and focus of the assessment schedule we have chosen to apply to a particular child.

It has already been discussed that the assessment process is not about secrets – so it follows that care planners and providers have to be honest about the purpose of an individual care plan.

Case study

Jay Tee Reynolds

Jay Tee is two. He is the youngest of the Reynolds children – he has four sisters: Jodie who is nine, Leah who is seven and the twins Shannon and Kelsie who are six. Jay Tee has Down's syndrome which was confirmed at six weeks. He is a happy two-year-old and well integrated into family life. Jay Tee is pre-verbal, but his sisters interpret well for him, so he never misses out. As of yet he has made no attempt to walk – but is content to shuffle on his bottom. Jay Tee will use the toilet if taken, but his family find life easier if he wears nappies. Mrs Reynolds has his name down for a local playschool, where the girls all went, but he must be out of nappies before he can go.

Physically Jay Tee is well, although he is overweight, due mainly to his inactivity and the fact that he spends most afternoons with his grandparents who own the local newsagents!

The Reynolds family have booked a family holiday to Florida this summer. Mr Reynolds is determined Jay Tee will be able to swim before they go.

Activity

List all the areas of shortfall as you see them in Jay Tee's life; now prioritise them. Reflect upon what you think other family members would consider to be the priorities for him; are there any differences? In your experience whose opinion would take priority?

It was important for us, in the early stages of 'Hello, this is me', to have a theoretical springboard to act as our catalyst for change – and while activity of living models of nursing (Roper *et al.* 1983) and life story book philosophies (Hewitt 2000) provided the start point for the assessment schedule a developmental theory was required to provide some sequencing for the prioritising process of planning.

It has long been accepted good practice to set a long-term goal for an individual and work towards its achievement through small graduated steps – but how do you decide what is the priority? A good starting place is always the achievement of 'normal' developmental milestones; but this relies on a distanced and detached decision being made on what a child should do next.

'Hello, this is me' has as a basic tenet the belief that having a disability is ordinary for both an individual child and their family; once we move that child into an outside care arena then living with that disability becomes the out of the ordinary, which compounds the description of developmental delay rather than identifying developmental needs.

Vygotsky (1978) in his discussions on human development puts forward the suggestion that the individual's ability to think and reason independently is the result of a fundamental social process. Vygotsky further suggests that we begin life as social beings, and are capable of interacting with others, but are unable to undertake physical or intellectual tasks independently – but that as children grow and are given opportunities to develop in all spheres (physical, social, psychological, cultural, emotional, spiritual, and cognitive) they move towards self-sufficiency and independence. It then follows that the more social opportunities children are given and activities they take part in, the more rounded and competent an individual they become, learning how to problem solve and interact effectively with their environment.

Vygotsky's concept of *the zone of proximal (or potential) development* (ZPD) holds great importance when the philosophies underpinning 'Hello, this is me' are reviewed. 'The zone of proximal development defines those functions that have not yet matured but are in the process of maturation, functions that will mature tomorrow' (Vygotsky 1978, p.102).

The child with a learning disability is often denied social experience that their peer group take for granted, particularly when they are described by what they cannot do – and not given opportunities to achieve and be measured by what they can do. By listening to parents and finding out what is ordinary for an individual child care environments are able to ensure that children can succeed and retain their dignity through their own levels of independence. By acknowledging that children who have a learning disability grow up, and matching experiences to their age group, we give these children opportunities to develop grown-up skills and life strategies.

The child   Opportunity   Experience   A life!

Figure 4.2 Living a life

It would be remiss to leave out of these discussions the fact that not only can the professionals' perception of the child and their lifestyle be at variance with the grown-up independence process, but so also can that of the child's parents.

In the last ten years all major government legislation relating to children has talked about the need for children with any sort of disability to be recognised as being children first, their disability being secondary to who they are as a person; it therefore follows that the concept of the eternal child (Wolfensberger 1972) has to be addressed and that plans must ensure that growing up is a right.

Anyway we agreed to give it a chance – after all, we'd tried every other hare-brained scheme that had been put our way – but this one was a revelation; all sorts of requests came – can she take some make-up with her? Didn't we use a cleanser, toner and moisturiser? She was even sent home with posters for her room.

I had to admit there was a change in Isabel, she looked different. I had to go and buy her some clothes because she looked too much of a baby in the ones she had before, and she really got excited when the radio was on. It seemed like she really could take notice for once.

Sammy (she's my niece, she and Isabel are the same age) came round. 'Glad to see your mum's let you join the land of the living,' she says to Isabel, and she took Isabel off to the park, both of them giggling. I bet a lad was involved! Dave, that's my husband, said to me, 'The thing is, doll, she'll never get a job, but she can grow up and we've got to let her.' You see, I never thought she could grow up.

Achievable goals and partnerships

It is important that before the process of 'Hello, this is me' moves any further the whole concept of achievable goals and partnerships is reviewed. In 1997 the Mental Health Foundation in association with Barnardos undertook an important piece of research called *Don't Forget Us*. Chapter 3 of this work discusses the development of community-based services and family support. Within the core recommendations is stated:

> The planning and provision of services should take into account the needs of the whole family and the possible impact of any interventions on other family members such as siblings, particularly where interventions are home-based. (Mental Health Foundation 1997, p.24)

When the concept of partnership is reviewed this is of particular importance, primarily as the whole notion of partnership has to be genuine rather than 'lip service' to a modern philosophy.

'Hello, this is me' relies on the notion of partnership not only with the parents but also with the child, brothers and sisters, important people in the child's life and other professionals. Children who have a learning disability only access respite for a fraction of their lives. Boundaries that relate not only to societal norms but also to those of the family of origin need to be considered, with particular reference to partnerships and common goals. This again makes it important for people (care providers and all family members) to acknowledge that the child with a learning disability is a person in their own right and is growing up fast!

All too often siblings of children who are 'just different' talk about their feelings of isolation and the belief that the world revolves around their brother or sister just because they have a disability. Professional interventions should be aimed at supporting extended family links that provide optimum life opportunities for personal growth and development for all family members, not just those who are 'just different'.

A goal-directed approach – Aiming for success!

For the model to have any real impact on the lives of children who access respite services the whole notion of goal setting needs to be addressed:

- Goals need to be achievable.

- Goals need to be realistic.

- Goals must be set in partnership.

- Goals must have a purpose.

- Goals lead to independence.

The model incorporates into the plan of care for each child a goal-directed approach that follows an individual child from home, to school, to respite and back again. As previously stated, if the model is utilised appropriately then parents are directors of care with their child, paid carers the enhancers.

Goals are often referred to as the aims of care – or the desired end result – or even hopes and wishes. Whatever you choose to call them, goals have common elements:

- Goals clearly state what an individual is working towards.

- Goals also state what we will be able to see which demonstrates the goal has been achieved.

- Goals tell us the conditions that will be in place to measure that a goal has been achieved.

- Goals tell us what the measurement of success is.

- Goals set time limits for when the goal is expected to be achieved.

It is our experience that goals are used and abused in care mainly because they are unattainable – not only does the child become disillusioned and bored but so do parents and carers. The setting of specific goals is a good example of how we measure children with a learning disability by what they cannot do, and set goals that reinforce this and compound the label of 'never will do'.

If we promote the broad aim of care as independence this then gives all involved in the child's care direction in drawing up specific goals. This process is often referred to as goal stepping.

Case study

Tyler Robinson

Tyler is 12; he has a moderate learning disability and uses his personality forcibly to get his own way. He lives at home with his parents and two sisters. Tyler's behaviour as of late has impacted on the way his family offers him opportunity. Tyler has a routine of inappropriate behaviours designed to manipulate a situation to his own advantage. Tyler's main triggers are family outings that do not revolve around him – for example, the weekly supermarket trip. Tyler's undesirable behaviour includes swearing, spitting at members of the public, pulling his sisters' hair, hitting his mother, screaming and self-harm – he bites the backs of his hands and draws blood. Mr Robinson avoids confrontation and chooses not to go out with the family. Mrs Robinson is much more determined that Tyler will learn to behave in a more appropriate grown-up manner. Tyler's sisters, Katrina and Lauren, who are 16 and 14, support their mother.

LONG-TERM GOAL

Tyler will behave in an appropriate way in public situations.

STEP ONE

Tyler will accompany his family on the weekly shopping trip each Saturday morning. He and his father will help choose the meat and vegetables for Sunday lunch, and then wait for the family in the café. To be reviewed in three weeks.

STEP TWO

Tyler is to take more responsibility during the family shopping trip. After he has helped to choose the meat and vegetables and had a milkshake, he and his father will rejoin the rest of the family to pay and pack the shopping. To be reviewed in three weeks.

STEP THREE

On Saturday morning Tyler is to help write the family shopping list. Six items are to be allocated as his special responsibility to fetch from the shelves. Tyler is to be supported in completing his tasks by his mother. After all the shopping is bought and paid for, Tyler and his family will have a drink in the café. To be reviewed in one month.

Activity

Think of a long-term goal for a child in whose care you have a lot of input – now step it into manageable and achievable components.

Selecting goals and establishing priorities

If the model is used as it was intended – that is, measuring children by what they can do and encouraging parents to describe what is ordinary for their child – then professional knowledge will enhance the goal selection process rather than dictate it. After all, in the independence process/continuum family norms and values need to be considered.

Reflect on the case study of Rebecca Westbury. The staff that care for her at respite have a perception of her disability that is at variance with that of her parents; this being so, each would select different goals for Rebecca which might include:

- increased integration

- development of self-awareness

- co-operation at meal times

- development of an acceptable sleep pattern.

But what would Rebecca's hopes for herself be? Most of the problems identified by the staff in the respite environment could be solved for Rebecca if there was open and honest dialogue between her carers and parents. This being the case, increased self-awareness, more integration and friendship would be beneficial and appropriate priorities for an eight-year-old little girl.

CHAPTER 5

Implementation

Care needs to be effective in its delivery and appropriate to the individual's current situation. 'Show me how and I might remember, tell me how and I might understand, but let me have a go as well and I'll learn.'

As has been previously discussed, the need to reflect relevance in an individual's life in care planning is important. Care plans need not only to reflect the changing needs of the individual, but also to be workable away from a professionally led environment; it is no good expecting to bring parents on board with the implementation of a care plan that needs the resources found in the respite setting. The efficacy of this sort of a plan in a child's life needs to be addressed. When the philosophical structures of 'Hello, this is me' were put in place the need for consistent transferability of care was considered. All too often care plans had been unsuccessful because of a number of issues:

1. Relevance. In nursing the need for the client to 'own' and be able to recognise the care issue/problem has long since been recognised. We felt that often in respite the suggestion was that a problem encountered in relation to everyday living skills was a problem shared in all spheres of a child's life, rather than any

consideration being given to how this aspect of the child's life fits into the family structure.

2. Resources. Many care plans we reviewed needed the support of a staff team to be implemented successfully, and were therefore not relevant to home, where maybe there were two other children, working parents and lives to live. The need to apply common sense in our philosophy was then evident, creativity, co-operation and communication being the route to success!

3. Reinforcers. Behaviourists acknowledge that success on any programme can depend on the selection of the right reinforcer. We needed to identify the most appropriate, that is easily transferable from home to school and respite and doesn't lose its efficacy.

Case study

David Koval

David is nine; he lives in a two-bedroomed housing association bungalow with his parents and younger brother Mark who is seven. The Kovals are refugees from Kosovo and have been in this country for approximately 18 months. David has a moderate learning disability, which is characterised by autistic tendencies and hyperactivity, and compounded by the fact that he speaks and understands little English. David attends a local special school five mornings a week, and joins a group of his peers from the refugee community during the afternoons for English lessons. David is to be excluded from these due to his hyperactivity and destructive behaviour. David's brother has a good command of the English language, and his mother often relies on him to translate when professionals visit. Mr Koval speaks very good English, but does not consider it a priority for David, or appropriate to be spoken in the home. David is a very frustrated young lad, who is isolated from his peers, and more increasingly from his family as he is not allowed out to play with Mark in the local street and park due to his bad behaviour. Respite has been arranged for David and an initial assessment is to be carried out at school where Mrs Koval will be supported by an official translator. Mr Koval says he cannot afford the time off work to attend the meeting and that the children are his wife's responsibility. David's behaviour at home is 'corrected' by his isolation; this has a negative effect on both David and Mark, especially as David 'trashes' the room most days, destroying Mark's possessions as well as his own. The school he attends has the facilities for a four-nights-a-week boarding arrangement; this has been suggested to the family, but Mr Koval will not consider it. He has only just begun to recognise the need for any professional help with David's care.

Activity

Identify what you believe are the areas of need in David's care. Prioritise them, and discuss them with a colleague or friend. Where do you feel the most resistance will come from, should a programme be drawn up addressing your priorities?

To implement effective care, the need to strengthen and build upon therapeutic alliances has to be considered. It is easy for a professional carer to see the way forward for an individual child, but in order to promote independence children need to have the path clearly mapped for them, with pitfalls marked and a consistent support network prepared. Children need to know why it is that care is being delivered and scheduled in a particular way, and more importantly that everyone is working towards the same goal.

Planning care delivery

Up until now all that we have written about supports the belief that caring for anyone with a learning disability is about providing opportunity and, while reluctant to put a numerical notion onto care (either cost or time), we see that without the appropriate staff framework in place opportunity and individual time is often misplaced amongst task allocation and reactive approaches to care. For the model to bring about maximum change and opportunity a review needs to take place of how work is allocated and organised. An individualised assessment based on a numerical scale, such as 'This is me', supports such a review and implementation process. (See Chapter 2 and Appendix 1.) All too often a minimum staff to child ratio relates to actual people in the building regardless of the care needs that individuals bring with them.

Utilising key workers effectively

We know Caitlin a lot better now; she's a real friend not just to us, but also to Isabel, and understands her really well. It was really upsetting when she came to tell us about the sort of service Isabel received and how they all wanted to change, you see although I hadn't wanted to think about her growing up, neither did I want to think of her spending her time in respite with little kids, and that's what had happened, a fluke really, it's just that a lot of six- and seven-year-olds were always booked in at the same time as her. It's different now. We worked together to get to Isabel's independence score, this means that her respite can be planned to make sure she gets the right amount of help to be as independent as she is able, and also that she can be with kids her own age and with similar abilities (that makes a nice change from saying 'similar disabilities'!). It wasn't all plain sailing, oh no, there were things Caitlin thought she knew about Isabel that she had to be put right on, like settling her at night, and her fits, but I suppose I had never passed on all the information, because it was as plain as the nose on my face so I thought everyone would know! At the end of the day Isabel has an independence rating of 90, I know that means she has a low level of independence, but it does recognise that she has some. We were also able to agree on the goals for her care for the next year. I think that this time next year her independence level will be moderate; now won't that be something to celebrate?

The role and function of the key worker

Whether the model is implemented in health or social care settings, one commonality will be the allocation of a key worker to each child who is in receipt of care. The label 'key worker' is often over-used and misused but it describes an important role in the caring team. It is our contention that if implemented effectively this role will enhance the life of the child, facilitate open and two-way communication channels between home and respite, and most importantly promote independence.

What is a key worker?

A key worker is a skilled and professionally trained adult carer whose responsibilities primarily relate to the assessment of the child, planning in partnership the aims of the child's care, facilitating the effective implementation of the child's care, and the evaluation of that child's individual programme of care. This skilled carer could be a nurse, a teacher, or a social worker; whatever the person's professional qualifications, they need to be able to accept responsibility for the care that is delivered to the individual child. The roles of the key worker are multifarious but a central theme, regardless of which agency that person is employed by, relates to the key worker providing a vital communication link between the child, his or her family and the care delivery service.

The roles of the key worker in relation to the model

1. To take a special interest in the child.

2. To build a working relationship with the child's family of origin.

3. To undertake the assessment of the child.

4. To set priority targets and goals in partnership with the child and family.

5. To communicate the agreed plan of care with all who are involved in the child's care.

6. To ensure the child's care is implemented effectively.

7. To provide a diary of events for the child to share with his or her family.

8. To represent the views of the child in planning goals.

9. To co-ordinate the evaluation of the child's care, and communicate the results of this review with all involved in the child's care.

10. To ensure that re-assessment takes place at least once a year.

11. To ensure that the child is cared for as a child first and foremost, any disability being secondary to who they are as a person.

No one person can effectively care for an individual child in the respite setting, and we would recommend the reader return to the independency criteria section of this book (Chapter 2). The success of the key worker concept relies on a cohesive network of associate workers to support the delivery of care and scaffold the child's development.

Care scenario

Peter is a registered nurse for people who have a learning disability (RNLD). He is employed as a senior care staff member by an independent sector establishment providing residential respite care for children who have a learning disability. He has a specialist interest in the care of adolescents who have mild disabilities. He is key worker for James who is 14, and Andy who is 15.

Peter works in a care team that comprises him, three other senior care staff members per shift, and a complement of six care support workers. In that team two care support workers support Peter in the delivery of James and Andy's care, if they are scheduled to be in respite.

Chikwan is a qualified social worker (Dip. SW) who is employed in the same home; she has a specialist interest in the care of young people who have multiple impairments. She is key worker for Sara who is nine and Martin who is 13. Two care support workers support Chikwan in the delivery of Sara and Martin's care, if they are scheduled to be in respite.

Peter and Chikwan each act as associate key worker for the children the other has responsibility for, when the other is not on duty. It is the associate key worker's responsibility to ensure that the care of these children is implemented as effectively as if the key worker were there, and that accurate records of the care they have received during that period are maintained, and passed on from one to the other.

All four sets of parents have met the two teams of staff and are happy that they contribute to their child's care and development.

Activity

Make yourself a list of the good and bad points of the way care is implemented in the respite care areas you have knowledge of. What would you like to change and why? What would you keep the same and why?

Care plans

The following care plans relate to the case studies used to illustrate points and act as a trigger for your thoughts.

Each plan is agreed by the parents and key worker, then signed and dated.

Care plan for Rebecca Westbury

After a detailed home assessment it has been agreed to ensure that Rebecca's routine for bed while in respite matches as near as possible her routine at home. Rebecca receives respite every Thursday and Friday evening during term time; she arrives straight from school at around 4.15pm.

Key worker appointed.

'Hello, this is me' assessment undertaken.

Goals agreed and care plan drawn up.

The aim of Rebecca's care: for her night-time care and routine to match as nearly as possible that of home.

PLAN TO MEET THE AIM

Rebecca has a 'This is me' independence rating of 91. This equates to a low level of independence as she has extra special care needs, and when away from her home environment needs the skills of a specialised adult carer to promote her personhood. Her night-time independence rating is 10 as she needs support both to get to sleep and to remain comfortable during the night.

Each evening at around 6.45pm, Rebecca is to be taken for her bath. She likes the bath to be warm and full of bubbles. She has her hair washed in the bath each evening. Her bath usually takes 15 minutes. Please wrap her in her towelling robe, take her to the yellow bedroom to be dried and apply body lotion. When she is dry, brush her hair and braid it loosely (this minimises the tangles for the morning). Rebecca needs you to clean her teeth for her, she uses a vibrating toothbrush and mint toothpaste, all her toiletries are in her bag which has been packed by her mum. Rebecca wears an attends during the night, she does not like a bedtime drink. Rebecca likes to start the night laid on her back. She likes the quilt to be loose around her and needs a safety guard on the side of her bed. She prefers a carer to sit with her for a few minutes while she snuggles down, and then please read her a chapter of whichever book her mum and dad have sent in. When the chapter is over, tell Rebecca you are going downstairs and wish her a good night, she likes the night light on, and a classical CD played quietly. Check Rebecca in 15 minutes, if she is not asleep, sit and stroke her hand for a few minutes to reassure her of your presence, leave her to fall asleep. This is usually enough support to get to sleep. Check Rebecca at regular 15-minute intervals to ensure she is asleep.

Rebecca requires turning twice nightly. She must be turned between 12 midnight and 12.15am and again between 3am and 3.15am. As Rebecca is a slight child, this only requires one carer and the minimum of fuss. Gently turn back the quilt, and while whispering reassurance turn Rebecca onto her left or right side, cover her up loosely, replace the safety guard, and leave her room.

In the morning Rebecca's ordinary routine involves being downstairs by 5.30am – this is not a problem. Monitor Rebecca for signs of wakefulness from approximately 5am. When she is sufficiently awake dress her in dressing gown and slippers and bring her downstairs. Her attends will need changing, and she likes her teeth to be brushed before she has her cup of tea.

Rebecca prefers a cup of tea with two sugars and full fat milk to be poured over a rusk which her parents supply. After her cup of tea Rebecca will happily sit by the French windows watching the world wake up, especially if you put a talking book on for her.

To be reviewed in four weeks.

Care plan for Melissa-Jayne McGinty

Melissa-Jayne is 18, and about to leave school. It has been agreed that she will spend the majority of the six-week summer holiday at Beach House for respite, while her family reach a decision regarding her continuing care. Melissa-Jayne has received respite within the service before, as a young child, and is known to several of the support staff.

> 'Hello, this is me' assessment completed both at home and with her key worker from the residential school. Startling differences noted.

> A key worker has been appointed, and is beginning to form a relationship with Melissa-Jayne's family.

> The goals of Melissa-Jayne's care have been agreed.

Aim of care: to provide Melissa-Jayne with a safe and stimulating environment from which she can maintain her relationship with her family, but also grow and develop.

STEP 1

Melissa-Jayne is to be introduced to the Beach House environment by her sister Corrine, on her way home from school next Friday. Amanda Jones (key worker) will be on duty to meet the sisters, and also to visit the family home the next day.

STEP 2

Melissa-Jayne will return to Beach House on Thursday evening from school, and spend the night and next day with her key worker. Mr and Mrs McGinty have been invited to come to tea and collect Melissa-Jayne on Friday at 4pm.

STEP 3

Melissa-Jayne only has three weeks of term time left. As Beach House is on a regular taxi run to her school, it has been agreed that she will move into her room at Beach House on Sunday, 1 July. Her family will bring her, and help her unpack. A welcome barbecue has been planned, and invitations sent out.

REVIEW

Melissa-Jayne has now resided at Beach House for two weeks. Her parents ring every evening to check on her day. Melissa-Jayne has settled well. She is resistant of physical contact, but tolerant of individuals who do not invade her space. She has an extra special care needs score of over 100, which means that she is dependent on others, and requires the support of a skilled adult carer to facilitate her life skills. It is hoped that Melissa-Jayne's stay will be extended to enable her to join the permanent group of young people who live at 17 Monks Road. The family have agreed that her older sister Corrine is the best advocate for Melissa-Jayne, and therefore will liaise closely with her sister, her parents and Amanda the key worker.

LONG-TERM GOAL

For Melissa-Jayne to move into 17 Monks Road.

SHORT-TERM GOALS

1. For Melissa-Jayne's parents to be accepting of her right to live away from the family home.

2. To compile a detailed 'Hello, this is me' assessment, from family knowledge and staff observations.

To be reviewed in six weeks.

Care plan for Ray Livingston

Ray has regular respite for two weekends each month. The initial request was to enable his sisters to spend some time with their parents, but Ray's respite now has some focus on benefiting him. On the first and third Friday of each month a 'lads' night' is run at the respite setting. This allows Ray to let off steam with a peer group, all of whom have similar abilities, and a personal development workshop is run on each of the following Saturday mornings for 45 minutes which explores self-concept and body image, growing up, tempers, falling out with family, and sexuality.

Key worker appointed.

'Hello, this is me' home assessment undertaken.

Targets for care agreed with parents.

Reinforcer identified – a game of pool with his dad once a week on a Sunday afternoon.

Goals agreed and care plan drawn up.

The aim of Ray's care: to provide Ray with the opportunity to identify with a peer group, and learn a more 'grown-up' strategy for expressing his own sexuality.

PLAN TO MEET THE AIM

At the moment Ray has learnt a series of sexually explicit phrases and behaviours that are designed to shock, for example masturbating in public and asking complete strangers to show intimate body parts. Ray needs to learn how to express his own sexuality in an appropriate way. He has few friends, as his home life is restrictive as his family are concerned that he is open to abuse through his eagerness to comply with promiscuous behaviours.

WEEK 1

Ray's respite arrangements have been altered; he will now arrive from home to respite at 6pm on alternate Fridays (the first and third of the month). Ray will be introduced to the other lads who take part in these 'nights in', and shown to his room. Ray will be asked to join in the planning of the evening, and his preferences noted. To be reviewed after his second visit.

WEEK 5

Ray prefers to play football, and listen to music with David and Rahnjit; he is to be invited to join the social skills group that is running the next day. The ground rules of the group are to be explained to Ray, and a contract drawn up between him and his key worker regarding 'grown-up behaviours'. This Sunday Mr Livingston will collect Ray before lunch and take him for a game of pool; it will be explained to Ray that this is the reward for grown-up behaviour.

WEEK 7

As part of his contract Ray has to report back to the group when he has used a behaviour that is not considered grown-up, and discuss with the group and his key worker why he used that strategy or behaviour. To be reviewed in four weeks, when Ray will invite his father to a review of what he has learnt.

Care plan for Jay Tee Reynolds

Respite has been requested for Jay Tee two afternoons a week between 2pm and 7.30pm. The reason for the request is to enable Mrs Reynolds to return to work, and also to provide help and support with Jay Tee's toilet training.

> Jay Tee will attend each Tuesday and Wednesday, and take part in the playschool run by the Briar Patch.
>
> Key worker appointed.
>
> 'Hello, this is me' assessment undertaken in the family home.
>
> Goals agreed and care plan drawn up.

The aim of Jay Tee's care: to improve his independence by promoting continence.

PLAN TO MEET THE AIM

At the moment Jay Tee makes no effort to take himself to the toilet, although he will co-operate when taken and there is success usually 50 per cent of the time. His family still use nappies throughout the day and night for him.

WEEK I

Jay Tee will be taken to the toilet at regular intervals throughout the day. He will wear 'pull ups' as opposed to nappies. Each time he is taken to the toilet the MAKATON sign for the toilet will be reinforced and Jay Tee will be praised for sitting on the toilet. A discreet record of his use of the toilet will be kept with the aim of establishing his ordinary habit.

WEEK 2

It has been established that Jay Tee uses the toilet appropriately at approximately two-hourly intervals. He is to be taken to the toilet throughout the day, and praised for appropriate use. As in Week 1 Jay Tee will wear 'pull ups' and the sign for the toilet will be reinforced. To be reviewed in two weeks' time.

WEEK 3

This week Jay Tee's care plan will be extended to include asking him if he needs a 'wee wee', before he is taken. Mum and Dad are encouraging him to nod for 'yes' and shake his head for 'no'. As in previous weeks, praise is to be the reinforcer and Jay Tee will still wear 'pull ups'. To be reviewed in two weeks' time.

WEEK 4

Jay Tee's favourite television hero is Scooby Doo, and his parents have bought him 'big boy pants' with Scooby Doo on them. He now wears these instead of the 'pull ups'. His care plans continue as in Week 3, but Jay Tee now has the added incentive of keeping his 'big boy pants' dry.

Care planning is never easy, and we do not advocate that any of the care plans used in this text could or should be used as standardised templates. The intention is to provide you with the impetus to consider care plans you have written for, or had applied to, your child or a child you know.

CHAPTER 6

Evaluation

Individuals receive care that is appropriate to their current situation.

'Assessment' and 'evaluation' are often used as if they were interchangeable terms, and while it is important to acknowledge that there are commonalities between the two, we need to remember that both are separate parts of the care-planning process.

Assessment is the start of the care-planning process. Assessment gathers together all the information relating to an aspect of the child's life, and culminates with a statement of intent, which has goals and priorities set. Evaluation, on the other hand, can only take place when care aimed at achieving the desired goal has been delivered.

At the beginning of the 'Hello, this is me' process, the concept of ordinariness determines the type of data that is collected to establish the goals. When 'Hello, this is me' and its impact on a child's life is evaluated the data collected describes independence.

The important difference to remember is that accurate assessment tells us what a child can do. Effective care that is appropriately evaluated will demonstrate what the child has achieved and more importantly why and how.

Case study

Jodie Pink

Jodie is 11; she has a mild learning disability. Jodie has recently made the transition from a special school to a mainstream comprehensive, where a team of special education support staff supports her and ten other pupils throughout the school. For the last two years she has received after-school respite as both her parents work until 5pm. When she was little Jodie used a local child-minder, but if not closely supported Jodie runs off, and she has recently got into trouble with local shopkeepers for stealing; her parents found that the after-school club at the local respite facility provided them with more peace of mind, and gave Jodie a more structured environment. Consequently Jodie had few friends away from this environment. Senior school has been a revelation for Jodie; she is mixing with a totally different peer group, and learning new social skills. She has made two new friends, Natasha and Nina, both of whom live in the same village as her. A phone call was received today from the special needs co-ordinator, to say that Jodie could not be found when her taxi called to bring her home from school. Her parents have been informed. Nina's mother rings the school at 5pm to say that Jodie has come home with Nina and Natasha on the local bus.

When Jodie is reunited with her parents she tells them she is sick of being treated as if she has a disability and will not go back to respite ever again.

When you read the case study of Jodie the need to provide a flexible respite service is obvious, one that supports and scaffolds young people who have a learning disability in making transitions into grown-up life in the community, but if we were to evaluate what has happened to Jodie in the last 12 to 18 months, there is great potential for adding negative labels, rather than evaluating the service we actually provide for her.

The components of evaluation

Process, structure and outcome are the three main components of evaluation. At the outset this model started from a fundamental belief that if we begin to assess the impact of respite a child is receiving, we have a moral and professional duty or obligation to be honest in our intentions and proactive in our delivery; it follows that this honesty must continue through the evaluation of an individual child's care. It was our experience that while evaluation did take place, its efficacy was dubious, and the attention to detail at its best patchy. From a detailed evaluation the care team should be able to see how and why a particular care plan has succeeded, and if there has been little positive movement towards achieving the goal then the plan can be re-written. More importantly when a child succeeds and is attaining independence with a new skill the evaluation should celebrate that fact, and reflect the point in the independency criteria.

Case study

Emillia Milano

Emillia is seven and has severe learning disability. She communicates verbally using a few words, but prefers to use a combination of dragging the adult to what she wants, and if really 'pushed' some Makaton. Emillia has a great deal of personal living skill, which is reinforced by the fact that she is the youngest of six children, and her parents push them all towards independence. She accesses respite every third weekend for three nights; here she is a bit of a 'darling', particularly as she loves to be cuddled, and generally made a baby of. At home she dresses herself, with the assistance of her older sister Carla: at respite she co-operates passively while the staff dress her. At school, she resists any attempts at taking her clothes off, especially for PE or swimming. At home she plays quite happily alongside other children, although she will not play with them. At respite she needs the support of a skilled adult carer to ensure she is not left behind. At school, she is often removed from the situation when other children are boisterous around her, as she bites.

At home she eats only what she wants, while in respite she eats everything that she is offered. At school meal times are considered her favourite time in the school day.

At home she is often still awake at 10pm and crying to come downstairs. Her bedtime routine in respite starts with a bath and story at 8pm, followed by a warm drink, and being settled by a carer.

Evaluation of all three aspects of her life would show that Emillia is manipulating her environments to meet her own needs!

Process evaluation

This component of evaluation examines the child and their carer. The intention of process evaluation is to measure what the child does, and the care that is being given. For example, the process evaluation of Emillia's bedtime routine while in respite shows far more individual time given, and support in actually getting to sleep. On the other hand, while she is at home, she is put to bed at a set time, and offered little in the way of support to settle for the night; as a consequence Emillia cries, and does not achieve an acceptable sleep pattern most nights.

Structure evaluation

This aspect of evaluation approaches the task from a completely different angle, and is fundamental in the utilisation of 'This is me'. Structure evaluation is concerned with the environment in which the care is given. It takes into consideration how independent the child is and the amount of staff support that individual child needs. It feeds into staff/child ratios for optimum care, and is an effective tool to use at annual audit to demonstrate the need to maintain or increase the staff complement and skill mix.

Outcome evaluation

This is perhaps the most obvious aspect of evaluation, because it concentrates on the child, and how far they have moved towards the achievement of a particular goal statement. For example, the care plan of Jay Tee Reynolds has an aim: to improve independence by promoting continence. By the end of Week 6 Jay Tee may still not have become 100 per cent continent, but if he uses the toilet when taken and has infrequent accidents, outcome evaluation would record the positive moves he has made.

Remember the dialogue in Chapter 3 from Damien's mother? Read what she has to say about evaluating her son's care.

We stuck our heels in and Damien didn't go to Beach House – a miracle occurred and suddenly there was space for Damien to receive respite at the Briar Patch.

Before we started using our time Philip came out to see us – he is Damien's key worker. It was great – he spent all Sunday morning with us, asking about Damien's life and really what made us all five a family.

I told him all about my fears and anxieties and the girls were able to tell him stuff about their brother that I wouldn't even have begun to think of as important – you know, dead ordinary stuff – things like that when he comes home from school he likes to rush into the garden, whatever the weather – just a quick run and then off comes his coat and bag. If you stop him he gets quite distressed. Carmel thinks it is because he has claustrophobia on the bus!

We were able to write down routines for all parts of his life, from getting up to going to sleep, and all the bits in between. Damien was with us all the time, so Philip would always be able to see him as a *brother* and a *son*. Not just a big lad with challenging behaviour who thumps if he doesn't get his own way!

Philip helped us draw up goals for Damien's care both at the Briar Patch and at home. Philip asked, 'What do you think Damien would like to change about the way he lives his life?'

'Being on the school bus,' said Carmel.

'Washing,' said my husband.

'Vegetables,' said Claire.

'Always getting angry,' I said.

'Well,' said Philip, 'I haven't got a magic wand – but maybe we could work together to topple all of these just like a pile of dominoes.'

This is what we all agreed:

- ° Damien has the right to get angry when things don't go the way he expects, but he must learn that he can't use bad behaviour to always get what he wants.

- ° Damien does not like his shower in the morning. We think this is because he doesn't have enough time to himself before he has to get on the school bus. From now on Damien will have a bath or shower in the evening, just before he has to go to bed. We will create opportunity for him to be out and about in the garden or conservatory before the school bus arrives.

- Meal times need not be a battle. At 14 Damien is old enough to know what he likes (broccoli and peas), and what he doesn't (Brussels sprouts and carrots). As a family we need to respect those choices he has made.

- The school bus is a big problem for Damien, if he can't sit at the front, and if any of the other children are noisy, then he really 'kicks off'. School is only 1.4 miles away from home, well within walking distance – but we don't have the time to take and fetch him every morning and afternoon. As a long-term aim, we will explore the possibility of 'respite in the community' providing Damien with a partner to walk home with him each day. In the meantime, each Wednesday and Friday afternoon, his mum will collect Damien from school and walk home with him.

The first night he was away I was like 'an ill-sitting hen'. I kept wondering what he was doing – how school had gone – you know, the usual nosey mum stuff.

The next day when he got off the bus he rushed straight in – out of the back door and ran around the garden – then came in and went in every room. Once he was satisfied he took off his coat and asked for a drink.

When he was watching the television I unpacked his bag. There was a new chat book – Philip had written in all about his stay, what he had done, eaten, how he had slept – all the things I wanted to know but which Damien had neither the words nor signs to tell me. It was such a relief, so when it came round to his next overnight stay I filled in what we'd been up to – just ordinary stuff – spent a weekend with

Grandma at the seaside, decorated Damien's bedroom, bought a new 'Steps' CD.

You know Damien will always be a difficult lad to care for, but at least we all talk to each other, and know what the other is doing for and with him. We are all part of Damien's winning team.

To conclude, it is important that all who are involved in a child or young person's care acknowledge that evaluation is not the last step in the care-planning process – it is merely the next. After all once a child has mastered the next step in the independence process the care plans need to ensure that there is adequate opportunity to practise the skill and maintain the mastery – thus enhancing further the independence of each individual child.

Activity

Think about a child in whose life you have a large input. How often are skills taught, or behaviours changed, with no opportunity after the evaluation to practise or maintain the skill?

CHAPTER 7

Making the Model Work

The only way any model will work is if it is used and put to the test. This chapter provides the reader with the assessment sheets and other documents used in the 'This is me' model. We would suggest that you read it with the lifestyle of a particular child in mind; consider how independent that child is now, and how independent they could be with an appropriate care plan and staff support to meet that plan.

How to use the assessment schedule

This assessment schedule should only be used to find the amount of staff support a child needs to be assisted in the promotion of independence. Ratings should be given by both the child's key worker and primary carer. Then a comparison is made. It may be that solutions to independence issues in respite are readily available at home so do ask!

The schedule is divided into ten headings:

- Rest, sleep and night-time care

- Personal care

- Breathing

- Communication

- Emotional, spiritual and cultural needs

- Playing and learning

- Personhood (what I know about me)

- Maintaining safety

- Eating and drinking

- Out and about.

Each heading has listed a series of criteria that impact on the child's independence. Attached to each criterion is a numerical score. All criteria have a description of the sorts of things a child may do to demonstrate that they need extra support to remain independent in this area of their life. Some criteria have sub-headings for extra issues that compound the child's need for skilled adult support. For example, under communication (has a hearing impairment), if the child's hearing impairment is corrected using bi-lateral hearing aids the child scores two.

Once the child's score has been agreed upon by respite and home then not only can staff support be matched to that child's needs, but also the child can be grouped for care with a peer group that promotes their own identity.

Recent studies into the impact of respite care for children with learning disabilities highlight the frustration parents and other family members feel about not knowing what their son or daughter has done while in respite or whom they have spent their time with (Brodin and Paulin 1997; Day 1997; Flynn *et al.* 1995; Hubert 1991; McGill 1996; Minkes *et al.* 1994).

By completing the independency criteria with the family, and discussing exactly what that level of independence means, we are dispelling the myth that assessment is about secrets.

Children who have a learning disability often find it difficult to form friendships with others. Opportunities are not created, and attempts at forging relationships face problems due to poor communication and networking skills. Many children who attend special schools live in scattered geographical locations from their classroom peers, and also lack the 'words and signs' to ask if a friend can come home for tea or to play. Therefore their isolation is compounded, and while we acknowledge the need to socialise with children without disabilities we also see that children like to play with someone from their own school, who understands the same games and rhymes, knows the name of their teacher, and can understand them. By grouping children together appropriately for respite, friendships can be made and encouraged.

If the chat book is used to facilitate open, two-way communication between all aspects of the child's life, partnerships in caring, alongside friendships, are strengthened, and self-actualisation aimed for.

Rest, sleep and night-time care

NORMALLY SLEEPS WELL   1

    The child goes to bed when prompted or taken and settles with the minimum of fuss, for example a story and a cuddle, reassurance, prayers, and ordinary routine.

TAKES MORE THAN 15 MINUTES TO SETTLE   2

    This child requires the carer to remain with them in the bedroom until they are asleep.

CARE ROUTINE INCLUDES A SLEEP MANAGEMENT
PROGRAMME   3

    This child has a planned programme designed to promote sleep; the programme must be followed.

ISSUES OF PERSONAL SAFETY

    The child has epilepsy; they need the support of a monitoring device, and/or cot sides.   2

and/or

The child wanders and can open doors. They need
a great deal of support to remain safe.   2

ESSENTIAL CARE   3

This child has problems with mobility and needs
re-positioning during the night.

IS DRY THROUGHOUT THE NIGHT   1

This child does not need disturbing during the night.
She/he is dry or wears an inco pad.

NEEDS DISTURBING/LIFTING DURING THE NIGHT   2

This child's ordinary routine includes a nightly trip
to the toilet.

WAKES OCCASIONALLY DURING THE NIGHT   2

This child wakes and requires attention, for example a
drink, a cuddle, a change of bedclothes, infrequently
(less than twice during one stay).

HAS A VERY DISTURBED SLEEP PATTERN   3

This child requires a lot of intervention during the
night, for example they have more than two
wakeful episodes that are noisy before 5am.

Personal care

HAS LIMITED IDEA OF BEING HOT AND COLD   1

This child will occasionally initiate a change of clothes
due to their own body temperature.

NEEDS CLOTHING SELECTED   1

This child has no idea of the use of clothing to maintain
their own temperature.

TOTALLY DEPENDENT ON OTHERS FOR WASHING AND
DRESSING   2

This child needs one person to wash and dress him/her.

CO-OPERATES PASSIVELY WHEN BEING WASHED AND
DRESSED   1

This child offers support to the carer who is washing
and dressing him/her.

ORDINARY ROUTINE INCLUDES A STRUCTURED
PROGRAMME FOR WASHING AND DRESSING   3

This child is learning to wash and dress himself/herself.

REQUIRES SUPERVISION   1

This child needs reminding of personal care
and tidying up.

NEEDS HELP SHAVING

Supervision is required to complete the shave safely.   2

or

A carer is required to shave this young man.   2

NEEDS ASSISTANCE TO GO TO THE TOILET   1

This child will use the toilet, but only if taken
and placed on the bowl.

REQUIRES MANUAL ASSISTANCE TO GET
ONTO THE TOILET   2

The child will use a specialist toilet if an appropriate
lifting device assists him/her.

WEARS AN INCO PAD   1

This child wears pads 24 hours a day.

INDEPENDENT IN OWN TOILET NEEDS   1

   This child asks to use the toilet appropriately.

HAS REGULAR PERIODS AND NEEDS SUPPORT   3

   This girl needs help to maintain her hygiene
      and dignity.

ORDINARY ROUTINE INCLUDES A TOILET TRAINING
PROGRAMME   3

   This child will need one-to-one support to meet
      the goals of his/her care plan.

Breathing

HAS A MEDICALLY CONTROLLED BREATHING PROBLEM

   This child has asthma.   2

and/or

   This child is susceptible to chronic chest infections.   2

WARNING: THIS CHILD HAS ALLERGIES!   4

   Read this child's case notes.

Communication

HAS A HEARING IMPAIRMENT

   This child has no hearing and no sign language.   4

   or

   This child has limited hearing and uses gestures.   3

   or

   This child wears bi-lateral hearing aids and
      communicates using a recognised sign language.   2

HAS A VISUAL IMPAIRMENT

This child is blind.   4

or

This child has limited vision and wears glasses.   3

HAS AN ACCEPTABLE COMMUNICATION PATTERN   2

This child is able to make himself/herself understood and understands others. He/she uses language and expresses his/her emotions.

HAS MINOR COMMUNICATION DIFFICULTIES   3

This child uses words and/or gestures to express his/her needs and desires. He/she has limited understanding of what others say.

USES MAKATON PROFICIENTLY   2

This child uses up to ten signs accurately.

EXPRESSES DESIRES AND WISHES THROUGH BEHAVIOUR   4

This child uses forceful behaviour to communicate; read the child's personal care plan.

HAS NO VERBAL COMMUNICATION   4

This child requires the one-to-one assistance of an experienced specialised adult carer in order to ensure his/her needs are met.

Emotional, spiritual and cultural needs

HAPPY IN ORDINARY CIRCUMSTANCES   1

This child accepts respite care as part of his/her routine, and is normally content in himself/herself.

REQUIRES A COMFORTER 1

This child requires a personalised article to ensure his/her 'wholeness'.

HAS SPECIAL REQUIREMENTS BECAUSE OF FAMILY BELIEFS 3

Read this child's care plan.

SHOWS FRUSTRATION THROUGH TEMPER 3

This child gets easily frustrated and displays ordinary infantile rages.

REGULARLY DESTROYS CLOTHING, SOFT FURNISHINGS, AND TOYS 4

This child if left to his/her own devices will tear and bite his/her own clothing. He/she also destroys toys and soft furnishings.

SELF-INJURIOUS BEHAVIOUR 4

This child harms himself/herself. Read his/her personalised care plan.

ATTACKS OTHERS 4

This child cannot be left unsupervised around other children, as he/she attacks them.

Playing and learning

LOCALITY OF SCHOOL

This child does not attend school. 4

or

This child attends a local school (within a two-mile radius). 1

or

> This child attends an out-of-district school.   2

ABLE TO EXPLORE FOR THEMSELVES WITH
SUPERVISION   2

> This child displays ordinary curiosity.

MIXES WELL WITH OTHERS   1

> This child initiates and joins in games co-operatively.

NEEDS ENCOURAGEMENT AND DIRECTION TO PLAY   3

> This child requires others to initiate and maintain play.

REQUIRES A HIGH LEVEL OF SUPERVISION   4

> Without adult support this child would remain isolated
> and under-stimulated.

Personhood (what I know about me)

IS AWARE OF OWN IDENTITY   1

> This child knows his/her name and uses it.
> He/she is aware of himself/herself and others
> around him/her.

SHOWS LITTLE AWARENESS OF SELF AND OTHERS   4

> This child shows little recognition of his/her own
> name and is unaware of others around him/her.

DISPLAYS LITTLE OR NO AWARENESS OF OWN
SEXUALITY   4

> This child requires adults to encourage his expression
> of sexuality through gender-appropriate clothing
> and companions.

IS AWARE OF OWN SEXUALITY AND THAT OF OTHERS   3

This child knows the difference between boys and girls. He/she expresses their own sexuality.

IS SEXUALLY MATURE   4

This child has reached a level of sexual understanding and experiments with their own sexuality. He/she is unaware of the risks involved.

MASTURBATES IN INAPPROPRIATE ENVIRONMENT   4

This child will masturbate if left to his/her own devices.

Maintaining safety

HAS NO AWARENESS OF DANGER   4

This child needs constant supervision during waking hours and regular checking through the night to ensure his/her safety.

REQUIRES SUPERVISION

This child expresses ordinary curiosity and needs adult supervision.   2

and/or

This child has limited concept of road safety, but a good understanding of the word 'danger'.   3

HAS EPILEPSY

Tonic/Clonic seizures   4

and/or

Petit mal seizures   2

and/or

Absence seizures   2

AT RISK FROM STATUS EPILEPTICUS   4

Eating and drinking

INDEPENDENT BUT NEEDS ENCOURAGEMENT   2

This child eats his/her food independently, once it is
prepared for him/her. Minimal verbal prompts are
required.

NEEDS ASSISTANCE

This child needs the support of an adult to eat
his/her meal.   2

and/or

The spoon needs loading for him/her.   2

and/or

He/she needs constant encouragement.   3

and/or

He/she is on a structured feeding programme.   4

REQUIRES FEEDING   4

This child requires individual attention as he/she
is fed.

HAS A SPECIALISED ASSISTED FEEDING PROGRAMME   4

This child has a condition that requires a medically
prescribed assisted feeding programme.

WARNING: THIS CHILD CHOKES!   4

Read the personalised care plan. This child regularly
chokes at meal times.

Out and about

INDEPENDENT 1

This child manages stairs, both up and down.
He/she walks and runs with only ordinary stumbling.
He/she requires minimal support when outside.

REQUIRES ASSISTANCE 4

This child needs a carer to hold his/her hand while
he/she walks. He/she has no road sense.

USES A FRAME AND ASSISTANCE 3

This child walks with the aid of a mechanical device,
prescribed by the physiotherapist.

REQUIRES GUIDING 3

This child has a visual impairment and needs guiding.

NON-AMBULANT 4

This child requires expert moving and handling.

USES A BUGGY OUTSIDE THE BUILDING 4

This child is unable to walk long distances due to
either maturity-dependency or disability.

'This is me'

Independence rating for

....

Compiled on

....

By ....

In partnership with ....

Overall level of independence equates to

....

Night-time extra special care needs

....

'This is me' independence rating runs out on

....

Agreed date for re-assessment

....

Signed .... Signed ....

Level of independence during the night

.... has an overall night-time presentation that has .... extra special care needs. This is because

....

....

....

Extra issues that need taking into consideration

Has a medically controlled breathing problem:

Has asthma	2
Is susceptible to chronic chest infections	2
Warning: This child has allergies!	4
Has no verbal communication	4
Expresses desires and wishes through behaviour	4
Has minor communication difficulties	3
Self-injurious behaviour	4
Attacks others	4
Regularly destroys clothing, soft furnishings, and toys	4

Has epilepsy:

Tonic/Clonic seizures	4
Petit mal seizures	2
Absence seizures	2
At risk from status epilepticus	4

Total night-time extra special care needs equates to ....
Assessed on ....

By .... in partnership with ....

No model is ever perfect, and all models have to be adapted to meet the needs of the particular parameters, societal and professional, in which the care is planned and delivered. In our evaluations to date of the model's implementation the impact on the lived experience of respite for a child is powerful. However, it is important to acknowledge that the independency criteria can give a skewed picture of the amount of support a child or group of children need during the night. Therefore we have included an extra sheet, entitled 'Level of independence during the night', that rates the support a particular child needs during the night; from this rating, an accurate staff to child ratio can be achieved during night-time hours.

To conclude, the authors would welcome the opportunity to work with organisations to implement both the model and the independency criteria, and any constructive comments that will lead to improved efficacy, which can only enhance the lives of children who have a learning disability and their families.

CHAPTER 8

Health and Social Policy

In considering the respite care of children with learning disabilities, which was the original focus of the work, we needed to consider both health and social policy in the United Kingdom. We knew from our anecdotal evidence that parents felt that there was little specialist provision for them. Often providers considered respite care as being 'only for the really bad cases' and not as a means of promoting the child's development, only as a service which gave the parent a break. This implied to parents that the mammoth job of caring for these special children was principally theirs and that the service would just give them a break to recharge their batteries if they got desperate.

The definition of respite care offered by Cohen and Warren (1985, p.26) is 'the temporary care of a disabled individual for the purpose of providing relief to the primary care giver'. Treneman *et al.* (1997, p.548) offer a definition of respite care as 'the shared care of a person with learning difficulties and/or physical disabilities, either at home or in a short-term residential setting, in order to give the family a break from the routine care taking'. The Mental Health Foundation (1997, p.23) offers the narrow definition of respite care as 'sending the child somewhere else (to another family, a residential care home or a hospital unit)'. Middleton (1999) suggests that 'respite' reinforces the idea that the disabled child is a problem for their family rather than an individual with their own needs.

Americans call respite care a 'gift of time' but the question is: for whom?

The role of parents in providing information to enhance a child's stay in respite, or their preparation for respite, has not always been recognised or encouraged (Oswin 1984). Oswin identified that short-term respite care was used for three main reasons:

- because of chronic problems in the family

- because of an emergency in the family

- because of a general need for parents to have occasional or regular support.

There have been many criticisms of the Children Act (1989) and its difficulties of identification of children in need. The language used in the Act definitions was open to interpretation and thus did not provide the kind of provision from local authorities that was originally envisioned by those who wanted changes. Although there is a great deal of improvement in terms of the management of child protection, this does not appear to be the same for children with special needs.

Historically respite care was offered in long-stay hospitals or in children's wards in district general hospitals. This denied children access to a mixed economy of care, and a more holistic service needed to be built. There is already a disinclination to treat these children as previously and a move away from giving children with special needs respite care within acute paediatric services or within long-stay institutions for children with learning disability. There was in many areas a lack of direction about what constituted a suitable alternative. Many believed the alternative was special foster parents who would work closely with families to provide respite services in a foster home situation. This form of respite, however, could prove to be costly for the foster family in terms of their commitment and the difficulty of saying no to requests for respite (Oswin 1984). Oswin also found that many social workers did not consider the foster family's feelings and often made unacceptable demands on them which could put their own family life in jeopardy.

The involvement of parents in the care has been a central part of the philosophy of children's nursing for some time, but it is important to learn that although we may feel we are working in partnership this may not be a view shared by the parents. This issue is discussed in Chapter 1. A recommendation made by the Mental Health Foundation (1997, p.24) is that the 'views and aspiration of families should inform all policy making, planning and service development'. They also suggest that short-term care should be provided with assessment, planning and review as integral components and that all of these should be individually arranged.

A few services have developed as a result of parent pressure such as for example Rose Garth. Parents identified the need and set about raising money to establish the respite centre. This gave an opportunity for parents to identify what they wanted to see from a respite service that was to be geared to their needs and reflect their feelings more. As with all services however there was always going to be an involvement of local government and health services to ensure that standards of care met acceptable standards. Because children with disabilities are seen as a long-term drain on resources with little likelihood of becoming contributors, much funding has been achieved by charities using pity and hoping for a sympathetic response (Middleton 1999). A view espoused by the disability movement is that 'rights not charity' should be the watchword (Middleton 1999). Treneman *et al.* (1997, p.553) state: 'Respite care should be regarded as a right and should be a positive experience for both child and family.'

The provision of services for children with learning disabilities covers many professional camps and philosophies. An aim of our model is to integrate communication which can improve the lot of some of these children and their families. In order to consider this we need to look at some of the history of the care of these children.

In the beginning of the child's life they are cared for by paediatricians in cases where difficulties are identified or predicted at birth and this begins the association of their parents with health services. Hall (1996) identifies that professionals often appear to be unaware of parents' concerns and that medical staff lack communication skills in giving diagnoses. How parents are told the news that a child may go on to develop long-term development delay is something which many agencies have been working to improve over recent years. Spearheaded by the 'Right from the Start' campaign led by the charity Scope an initiative was set up to improve the initial telling of parents and families. In this initial period parents will experience grief as they cope with the loss of the child that was expected and looked forward to, and will come to terms with the often complex and difficult needs of the child they have.

Many families' early experiences will be in neonatal units where children may spend several months hovering between life and death and where outcomes are difficult to predict and futures difficult to plan. The move between hospital setting and home can be a large step for these families as they begin to understand the daily commitment these children are going to demand. They may receive help from skilled neonatal community nurses who can support the early transition into the home setting and will often then be transferred to the care of paediatric community nurses who may continue to provide practical help. Future admissions to hospital may be required for children who have ongoing medical problems requiring attention. These may be co-ordinated by the same consultant paediatrician who has been involved from the beginning and so forms part of a link for parents with the beginning of their child's story.

Story telling is a part of a child's history which can prove complicated over time for parents particularly if new doctors and nurses come on to the scene who have not been involved from the beginning. Continual repetitive admission procedures can be honed down and communication can be enhanced to build ongoing relationships (Robinson 1987). Each new professional will bring their own personal interpretation of the story and this may not always fit well with the parents' own perceptions. Having a comprehensive story as part of our plan aims at having a clear identification of who the child is and what they can do rather than looking for problems. If this story is available to all who work with the child in a logical and reasonable amount of detail it should reduce the amount of misunderstanding that can occur. The difficulty can be in providing enough information at the right level for those who need it. It is our contention that if a comprehensive plan like this can be used from the beginning it will assist inter-agency working and if it is a contemporary record maintained by all who have input into the family it will provide an excellent record of the child's life. It is an extension of the family-held health records already used for all children but augments it with the extra information these children generate.

Children and their families may be referred to different agencies in connection with the different problems they may experience over time. For example, many will have social worker input from the beginning to provide extra resources they may need. Problems may arise to do with housing alterations required or financial problems due to an increased burden of care. Growing children mean increasing demands on carers and their resources, which can necessitate a social worker's help.

The input of physiotherapists, occupational therapists and portage workers adds to the number who are involved with the child. Many children may be referred to special education services by the time they are two years of age and so the number of professionals with an interest in the child grows. As this grows so does the complexity of providing seamless services which meet the needs of the child and family (Gravelle 1997). Gatford (1999) suggests that there is an evident need for a more comprehensive and cohesive assessment which looks at the child and the provision of services from one assessment rather than the multiple assessments which currently take place. This would involve a much greater co-operation between different disciplines than we presently see, with much less in the way of 'territorialisation'. In the report *Don't Forget Us* (Mental Health Foundation 1997) parents identified that they would value highly a 'properly co-ordinated, integrated teamwork approach' in the management of children with challenging behaviour. This can be applied to all disciplines. The value of working together cannot be denied and its importance should be noted by caring professionals.

Hall (1996) identified that an issue that provoked anxiety for mothers was the endless round of assessment required by professionals. One mother suggested that there should be one record which all have access to in order to prevent all the re-assessment which was happening. It was suggested that all professionals should use it with a user-friendly approach and a plan of care negotiated by parents and professionals. 'This is me' and 'Hello, this is me' are an attempt to offer such documentation as a supplement to the parent-held child health record in use for all children.

The difficulty of identifying who should pay for care is one that can cause problems. In the first two years in particular the parents are expected to provide for care, particularly as most children are totally dependent on parents for care at least until two years of age. However, if parents do not keep families together with children with severe disabilities or complex needs, who would provide that care? And how much would that cost? (See Gatford 1999.) Identification of a child's extra special needs may be prolonged and the cost of providing equipment needed may be met by different budgets at different times. This can be confusing for parents and health or social professionals alike. The need remains constant but the provider may change. While one purchaser may provide one brand, another may provide a different one. While the products may do the same job, changing brands may prove difficult for the parents who are used to one type. It is akin to telling a family after years of using Heinz baked beans that they now have to use a different brand. Perhaps the quality is the same but the taste is different. Anyone who has tried to change a brand with a child will know that this is not always a smooth or easy transition! It could be argued that agencies can make parents' lives more difficult by changing things that could stay the same, often in order to keep costs to a minimum. There are suggestions in recent reports that funding should enable some families to hold individual budgets if they want to (Department of Health 2000; Mental Health Foundation 1997) in order to purchase their own respite care.

Parents will differ in their expectations of health care provision and many will have high expectations that may not always be met in reality (Gravelle 1997). Services will be more effective the more they meet the individual needs of families (McGill 1996). In the work by McGill (1996) it was identified that there were often differences in perspectives of parents in terms of their expectations of the respite services. He suggests that the challenge of providing respite care when and where it is needed and in the way that individual families want it needs to be met. Families' needs may change and the service needs to be flexible to respond to new requirements for resources or support (Gravelle 1997).

The pressures of managing a budget are familiar to all; whether it is a multi-million pound budget or a family house-keeping budget essentially the same difficulties are found. Do you buy a more expensive product because it provides better value for money or do you always buy the cheapest – even if it is not the best? It is difficult for parents to accept that products supplied for their child may be provided because they are the cheapest – not because they are the best. Which parent does not want their child to receive the best that is available? Fighting for service provision for their children can often be as stressful as (or more than) caring for the children themselves (Gravelle 1997). Is it any wonder that many give up or prefer to struggle on alone because they cannot cope with the constant fighting to receive care (which we could argue should be a right)? Evidence suggests that respite care is valued by parents, enabling them to cope by alleviating stress (Treneman *et al.* 1997).

A further constraint felt by families can be that they feel that they have to provide for their own child and that there is some dishonour in asking for help. Many find it difficult to accept help from anyone as it is like accepting charity. Many would rather struggle to the point of collapse than admit that they cannot cope and that they need help. The first time they have to tell a professional that they cannot cope can be traumatic. Feelings of guilt and inadequacy are common, often accompanied by feelings of relief that they have admitted their difficulties (Folden and Coffman 1993). A common feeling described by parents is that they feel no one will care for their child like they do. They can find it hard to trust others and hard to believe their child will be happy (Treneman *et al.* 1997). Trust is developed through confidence that their decision to use respite is correct; this will lead to peace of mind which is important for relaxation and enjoyment to occur (Folden and Coffman 1993). Difficulty with trust is made worse by reports of carers who abuse trust and abuse those in their care. This difficulty can be increased if the carers providing respite care do not talk with parents and communicate their willingness to care for the child in the way the parents want and also their willingness to report back on a child's stay. The child and family-centred approach is discussed more in Chapter 1. This has an impact on the family from a health and social policy perspective because it may have an effect on the nature of respite care they demand. Why should families not expect a high standard of care for their child? The difficulties arise when we examine who is responsible for providing that care. Duff (1992) reports that parents often felt that they were not listened to enough or given opportunities to be consulted about service provision. Parents and service providers need to share similar viewpoints on why children behave as they do in order to work towards common goals. Duff (1992) also emphasises the importance of consistency between home, school and respite services in the care of children.

Socio-economic factors and family circumstances will affect a family's ability to provide care for a child with complex needs (Mental Health Foundation 1997).

Money will always be important as we examine care needs and look at the cost of providing such care. Our model tried to consider care provision from different perspectives, listening to parents and trying to provide child-centred care and also looking at the practicalities of provision of care. An attempt was made to balance a group of children having respite care with the carers who were available. This is not always straightforward to achieve. Within the model there had to be an element of flexibility in order to retain some elements of crisis intervention, such as when there is a sudden illness in the family, or some other family crisis requiring emergency respite care.

However, our belief is that if respite can be planned, can be demonstrated to be family/child-centred, and can give good feedback to parents demonstrating the child has been well cared for, this will lead to parental confidence in the service. This confidence in turn should lead to more effectively planned respite care rather than just a crisis intervention service. Planning for respite early can prevent parental exhaustion and burn-out (Campbell 1996; Gravelle 1997). Failure to do this can lead to a crisis admission for respite, which is not satisfactory for the child or the family. McGill (1996) reports on the importance of respite care to ensure children and adults remain with their natural families. He also suggests that respite services are often insufficient to cope with the demands of families and are inflexible.

The difficulty with only acting as a crisis intervention service and providing respite on demand is that respite is often unplanned so resources cannot easily be targeted. Also, the nature of crisis intervention is that it arises from a period of crisis which can hamper effective communication about the child's abilities and needs. The child's behaviour may be affected as a result of the crisis, which may also have affected the parents' behaviour and feelings. This makes respite stressful for the child and carers and can make it equally stressful for parents who feel they have let their child down by failing to cope with this crisis. The use made of respite care is influenced by stress levels and the degree of perceived support for families (Treneman et al. 1997).

Ideally respite should be planned to meet the child and family's need and purpose; however, it often looks only at the family's need. Respite care is now recognised as being a positive experience for the child as well as the family (Treneman et al. 1997). There is no doubt that families need respite care in order to continue to provide the ongoing care of children whose needs can be complex and demanding (Brodin and Paulin 1997). It can help parents to recharge batteries and reduce stress before a crisis ensues and this improves their individual health (Campbell 1996; Folden and Coffman 1993). Day (1997) suggests that short-term care should benefit children both through the assessment of physical needs, and also through the provision of social activities to assist social development. This view is endorsed by the findings of a survey looking at respite services for adults (Flynn et al. 1995).

In an ideal situation there will be time to plan for the respite. This time is needed for the family to plan, for the carers to plan for the child's visit and for the child to be prepared for the visit as much as possible. Planning can enhance respite because, for example, groups of school friends might be able to have respite together. When respite is planned carers can be organised to be available so that all children receive the support they need to maintain and develop their level of independence. The tendency to rush in and 'take over', by carers, can be tempered by the need to maintain and develop the child's independence. In planning respite care we should also meet the needs of children and their families with respect to their cultural identity (Folden and Coffman 1993).

McGill (1996) reminds us that more research has focused on the benefits of respite to the family than on the benefit to the child or adult receiving the care. It is our opinion that respite care should be a continuation of care that encourages the development of physical, emotional and social skills and that does not just 'baby sit'. Raised expectations enhance performance and the encouragement of children to continue development is important in their continued advancement – however slow that progress might be (Olshansky 1972).

The ability of staff to follow individual programmes for children can be affected by the number of children and carers within the unit at any one time (Oswin 1984). Also respite services are sometimes challenged as much as the family by the nature of challenging behaviour that the child or adult demonstrates (Lyon 1995). That is where training and monitoring of staff is important (Oswin 1984).

In the work by McGill (1996) parents were asked to comment on what they felt were important features of respite provision. Those identified were: locality, transport provision, organisation of service, degree of involvement with parents (parents wanted to have a say and be listened to by the service providers), organised activities for the children, staff make-up and the nature of others sharing respite with their child.

The long-term view needs to be considered when looking at the costs of care for those with extra special needs. In work by Brodin and Paulin (1997, p.202) a parent comments, 'If a child gets all possible help to develop and learn how to take care of himself, then society will save enormous sums of money when the child grows older.' Middleton (1999) suggests that respite should make a positive contribution to a child's development in the same way for all children regardless of disability. Minkes et al. (1994) suggest that sometimes the needs of the child need to be considered separately from those of their parents and family. Cherry and Carty (1986) place on children's advocates some of the responsibility of making society aware of the special developmental opportunities that children require in order to achieve their full potential as adults. This leads to social policy taking into account the need for children to have their development both monitored and promoted. The value in this model is that it focuses on independence and this will prove valuable to the child in their future life. It is also valuable to those financing care, as the greater independence these children achieve the less resources they are likely to need as adults. A parent quoted in the report *Don't Forget Us* (Mental Health Foundation 1997) says:

Children with learning disabilities and severely challenging behaviour may be seen as 'too complicated' and 'too expensive' by conventional children's services. But we love our children and see them as worthy of the best possible support. Also if we have to talk 'value for money', let's remember that there are social and economic costs to failing to make proper provision for challenging behaviour (p.9).

For many who reach adulthood resources of some kind will always be needed, but the less intensive the resources required, the cheaper the care will be for the provider. For the individual the value of their individuality will be enhanced and the value of their existence to themselves and others will be so much the richer as they are encouraged and enabled to achieve their full potential. Middleton (1999) emphasises that children are developing human beings who are continually changing. Within the developmental perspective it is recognised that all children are in need of 'a measure of protection, care and guidance' (Middleton 1999, p.122).

Gatford (1999) writes of how families caring for a child with severe or complex extra special needs may be socially excluded. This is because such care usually involves great changes to lifestyle. Planning 'normal' trips out can pose enormous challenges (Gravelle 1997). Pickard and Williams (1996) identify that parents can feel exposed as a result of coping with difficult behaviour in public and that many parents think that society views them as inadequate parents as they cannot control their child's behaviour. Many families may not realise what support is available. This information should be passed on by nurses and other professionals in contact with the family (Gatford 1999). Lack of information can limit the access parents have to respite services (Hall 1996).

Quality assurance of respite services can be maintained by adequate training and the supervision of volunteer carers (Folden and Coffman 1993). Parents' confidence in the abilities of those caring for their children is essential (Gravelle 1997). Treneman *et al.* (1997) identify that the active involvement of parents in planning and monitoring respite care will ensure that their needs are fully met.

The report *Don't Forget Us* identified some key issues that need to be addressed. They were: poor co-ordination of services, the need for central government policy about children, and the need for coherent and strategic approaches to services and staff training (Mental Health Foundation 1997). Poyser (2000) points out several problems that contribute to inadequate service provision: social isolation, financial problems, organisational constraints, difficulties with fulfilling the provision of the Children Act (1989), lack of continuity of care and fragmentation of services.

We would like to suggest that the commitment shown by staff using the model could be the catalyst for change and the springboard for success to begin to redress the imbalance in children's services.

CHAPTER 9

'Listen to Me, I am a Grown-Up!'

As care givers it was important for us to acknowledge the next step for our model. Logic dictated that this had to be the transition young people make into adult services, and while the care study and subsequent care plan for Melissa-Jayne McGinty (see Chapters 3 and 5) demonstrate how the philosophy could be used to establish the working partnership between the young person with extra special needs, their family and the paid carers, in our opinion it did not address the ordinariness of being an adult – for example, change in relationships, work, expectations and aspirations. It is important to remain cognisant of the fact that while underpinning philosophies that promote independence transcend age barriers, the headings of our independency criteria and care-planning schedule ('Hello, this is me') do not.

If people who have a learning disability are really going to 'move into the mainstream' (SSI 1998) then a service needs brokering that acknowledges the life they have already lived – and the expectations and aspirations they have as adults.

Wolfensberger (1972), in writing about the concept of deviance in human management services, uses social imagery to explore the concept of deviancy and the person with a learning disability. If positive lifestyles are to be promoted successfully for individuals who have a learning disability, then many of the myths and mistakes, with particular reference to negative labels acquired during childhood and adolescence, need to be examined.

The label of 'eternal child' (Wolfensberger 1972) is often given to adults who have a learning disability; it is our opinion that by facilitating a successful transition from one age band service to another and by offering people life maps that reflect their new adult status some of this negative imagery can be addressed. One example of negative imagery is the use of childish versions of names. Most of us have cringed in embarrassment when an older family member has called us the pet name of our childhood in public; think of the clients you have cared for whose names never grew up with them. Perhaps more importantly we need to consider the lost memories of individuals with a learning disability; 'hand-held health records' are becoming increasingly more commonplace for most members of the public, but what about a record of life that follows the person from one care setting to another, remains their own property (after all, it is their life we are reading and writing about), and is updated each year?

In 1998 the Social Services Inspectorate published its report *Moving into the Mainstream*, which reviewed eight local authority social services departments to see how effectively they carried out their duty of ensuring that people with a learning disability have the social care support they need. Their report acknowledges that, compared with the past, services now give:

- a bigger choice of where people can live, including supported housing and family placement schemes

- a wider range of day services and employment schemes and less reliance on old-style adult training centres

- more (but not enough) respite and shared care

- more services supporting people in their own homes

- more specialist services for people with additional disabilities and needs

- more use of education and college courses

- more use of recreation and leisure facilities

- more choice for people of different ages and with different interests.

(SSI 1998, p.1)

The report goes on to ask key questions of staff responsible for delivering care to individuals who have a learning disability. When the development of this model is considered to include young people making the transition from child to adult services, three questions go some way to raise the awareness of carers, families and young people with a learning disability about the concept of ordinariness, and about the need to establish a service that ensures the successful transition from one service to another:

- Have you sought users' and carers' views about their experience of moving from school into the new world of adult services?

- What was learned that could help other school leavers?

- Are care plans developed jointly with users, carers and other staff?

(SSI 1998, pp.11–13)

The model 'Listen to me, I am grown-up!', given at the end of this chapter, is designed to show that care planning is a living entity that grows and develops with the person to whom it belongs, but the paperwork needs to grow and develop with them.

Conclusion

This new century offers all sorts of exciting opportunities to the human race. Medical boundaries will be pushed, and the use and development of new technology could enhance everyone's lives. People with a learning disability should not be left behind. The brand new Human Rights Bill (2000), in our opinion, does not do enough to promote basic human values and rights for this group, and does not make planned care a basic right.

In one final reflection, ask yourself these questions:

1. When did you last ask a child with a learning disability what they wanted to do?

2. And more importantly did you listen to the answer?

3. How often have you seen a label applied to a child who has a learning disability because little attention has been paid to 'normal' human development?

4. Do children with a learning disability get recognised as having different needs from their family?

5. When did you last ask a child with a learning disability (or consider) what they most wanted to change about the way they live their life?

If children are to be empowered, if parents are to be partners, if carers are to be effective, then we all need to learn and accept that reflecting the concept of being ordinary is a skill that specialised adult carers need to learn, and parents acknowledge. Providers and planners need to listen, and ensure that education and opportunity are available to the specialised adult carer so that change can be a reality, and ordinariness just that – ordinary!

Hello, this is me

How do we see ourselves? And how does this relate to the way we wish to be cared for?

'Listen to me, I am a grown-up!'

Hello, my name is

....

I was born on

....

I live at

....
....

with

....
....

This booklet lets me tell you all about me.
I filled it in with

....

on

....

We will make a review of this year on

....

Important information about me
This is *confidential*

My full name is ....

I prefer you to call me ....

My home address is ....

Telephone number ....

The most important people in my life and their
relationship to me ....

....

....

My next of kin is .... and can be contacted at

....

During the day I ....

....

....

IMPORTANT MEDICAL INFORMATION
....

My GP is ....

What I need you to know about my health ....

....

More about me

For example, where I went to school, the respite I received, my biggest successes, my favourite holiday destinations.

Ordinary things that happen in my life

Sleeping

Waking up

Personal hygiene

Using the toilet

Eating and drinking

Weekdays

Relaxing

Having fun

Communicating

Being happy

Being sad

Showing frustration

Being with others

Spending money

Making my needs known

Being independent

Travelling

My favourite things

My bad habits

Weekends

Things I would like to change about the way
I live my life

Being out and about

What I know about me

Special information about my health

How I feel about respite

Admission sheet

I...................arrived today ....

at .... via ....

....

I am going to stay for ....

I came for respite because ....

....

I brought with me ....

....

....

I was met at the door by ....

....

I am staying in .... room, the other people who I

will be with are ....

....

The person who will be responsible for my care
while I am here is ....

....

We both agreed that I have ...... cuts and bruises

Any special information you need to know about
my stay this time, or to care for me this time

....

....

A record of my stay and the care I received

Care plan for ....

Aim

How are we going to reach that aim?

When are we going to review it?

Who else is to be involved in my care plan?.........
....
Please fill in daily how much progress I have
made towards my aim ....
....
....
....
....
....
....
Today is my review date. What have you got to
say about my care plan?.......................................
....
....
....
....
....

This is a review of all the things I have done with you in respite this year. Please remember that sometimes me and my friends do not have the words or the signs to tell people what a good time we have had, so include some pictures!

'This is Me'

Rest, sleep and night-time care

Normally sleeps well 1
The child goes to bed when prompted or taken and settles
with the minimum of fuss, for example a story and a cuddle,
reassurance, prayers and ordinary routine

Takes more than 15 minutes to settle 2
This child requires the carer to remain with them in the bedroom
until they are asleep

Care routine includes a sleep management programme 3
This child has a planned programme designed to promote
sleep; the programme must be followed

Issues of personal safety
This child has epilepsy; they need the support of a monitoring
device, and/or cot sides 2
This child wanders and can open doors. They need a great deal
of support to remain safe 2

Essential care 3
This child has problems with mobility and needs re-positioning
during the night

Is dry throughout the night 1
This child does not need disturbing during the night. She/he
is dry or wears an inco pad

Needs disturbing/lifting during the night 2
This child's ordinary routine includes a nightly trip to the toilet

Wakes occasionally during the night 2
This child wakes and requires attention, ie a drink, a cuddle,
a change of bedclothes, infrequently. Less than twice during one stay

Has a very disturbed sleep pattern   3
This child requires a lot of intervention during the night, for
    example they have more than two wakeful episodes that are noisy
    before 5am

Personal care

Has limited idea of being hot and cold   1
This child will occasionally initiate a change of clothes due
    to own body temperature

Needs clothing selected   1
This child has no idea of the use of clothing to maintain
    his/her own temperature

Totally dependent on others for washing and dressing   2
This child needs one person to wash and dress him/her

Cooperates passively when being washed and dressed   1
This child offers support to the carer who is washing and dressing
    him/her

Ordinary routine includes a structured   3
programme for washing and dressing
This child is learning to wash and dress himself/herself

Requires supervision   1
This child needs reminding of personal care and tidying up!

Needs help shaving   2
Supervision is required to complete the shave safely
or
A carer is required to shave this young man   2

Needs assistance to go to the toilet   1
This child will use the toilet, but only if taken and placed
    on the bowl

Requires manual assistance onto the toilet   2
The child will use a specialist toilet if an appropriate lifting device
    assists him/her

Wears an inco pad   1
This child wears pads 24 hours a day

Independent in own toilet needs   1
This child asks to use the toilet appropriately

Has regular periods and needs support   3
This girl needs help to maintain her hygiene and dignity

Ordinary routine includes a toilet training programme   3
This child will need one-to-one support to meet the goals of his/her
    care plan

Breathing

Has a medically controlled breathing problem   4
This child has asthma   2
and/or
This child is susceptible to chronic chest infections   2

Warning this child has allergies!!!!   4
Read this child's case notes

Communication

Has a hearing impairment
This child has no hearing and no sign language   4
or
This child has limited hearing and uses gesture   3
or
This child wears bi-lateral hearing aids and communicates using a
    recognised sign language   2

Has a visual impairment
This child is blind   4
or
This child has limited vision and wears glasses   3

Has an acceptable communication pattern   2
This child is able to make himself understood and understands others.
    He/she uses language and expresses his/her emotions

Has minor communication difficulties   3
This child uses words and or gesture to express his needs and desires.
    He/she has limited understanding of what others say

Uses Makaton proficiently   2
This child uses up to 10 signs accurately

Expresses desires and wishes through behaviour   4
This child uses forceful behaviour to communicate. Read the child's
    personal care plan

Has no verbal communication
This child requires the one to one assistance of an experienced
    specialised adult carer in order to ensure his/her needs are met   4

Emotional, spiritual and cultural needs

Happy in ordinary circumstances   1
This child accepts respite care as part of his/her routine, is normally
    content in himself/herself

Requires a comforter   1
This child requires a personalised article to ensure his/her
    'wholeness'

Has special requirements because of family beliefs   3
Read this child's care plan

Shows frustration through temper   3
This child gets easily frustrated and displays ordinary infantile rages

Regularly destroys clothing, soft furnishings and toys   4
This child if left to his own devices will tear and bite own clothing.
    He/she also destroys toys and soft furnishings

Self-injurious behaviour   4
This child harms himself/herself. Read personalised care plan

Attacks others   4
This child cannot be left unsupervised around other children, as
    he/she attacks them

Playing and learning

Locality of school
This child does not attend school   4
or

| This child attends a local school (2-mile radius) | 1 |

or

| This child attends an out-of-district school | 2 |

Able to explore for themselves with supervision   2
This child displays ordinary curiosity

Mixes well with others   1
This child initiates and joins in games co-operatively

Needs encouragement and direction to play   3
This child requires others to initiate and maintain play

Requires a high level of supervision   4
Without adult support this child would remain isolated and under-
stimulated

Personhood (what I know about me)

Is aware of own identity   1
This child knows his/her name and uses it. He/she is aware of
himself/herself and others around him/her

Shows little awareness of self and others   4
This child shows little recognition of his/her own name and is
unaware of others around him/her

Displays little or no awareness of own sexuality   4
This child requires adults to encourage his/her expression of
sexuality through gender appropriate clothing and companions

Is aware of own sexuality and that of others   3
This child knows the difference between boys and girls. She/he
expresses their own sexuality

Is sexually mature   4
This child has reached a level of sexual understanding and
experiments with their own sexuality. Is unaware of the risks
involved

Masturbates in inappropriate environment   4
This child will masturbate if left to own devices

Maintaining safety

Has no awareness of danger   4
This child needs constant supervision during waking hours and
    regularly checking through the night to ensure his/her safety

Requires supervision   2
This child expresses ordinary curiosity and needs adult supervision
and/or
This child has limited concept of road safety, but a good
    understanding of the word DANGER!   3

Has epilepsy
Tonic/Clonic seizures   4
and/or
Petit Mal seizures   2
and/or
Absence seizures   2

At risk from status epilepticus   4

Eating and drinking

Independent but needs encouragement   2
This child eats his/her food independently, once it is prepared
    for them. Minimal verbal prompts required

Needs assistance   2
This child needs the support of an adult to eat his/her meal
and/or
The spoon needs loading for him/her   2
and/or
He/she needs constant encouragement   3
and/or
He/she is on a structured feeding programme   4

Requires feeding
This child requires individual attention as he/she is fed   4

Specialised assisted feeding programme   4
This child has a condition that requires a medically prescribed
    assisted feeding programme

Warning: this child chokes!   4

Read personalised care plan. This child regularly chokes at meal
   times

Out and about

Independence   1

This child manages stairs, both up and down. He/she walks
   and runs with only ordinary stumbling. He/she requires minimal
   support when outside

Requires assistance   4

This child needs a carer to hold his hand while he/she walks.
   He/she has no road sense

Uses a frame and assistance   3

This child walks with the aid of a mechanical device, prescribed by the
   physiotherapist

Requires guiding   3

Child has a visual impairment and needs guiding

Non-ambulant   4

This child requires expert moving and handling

Uses a buggy outside the building   4

This child is unable to walk long distances due to either
   maturity-dependency or disability

'This is me'

Independence rating for

....

Compiled on

....

By ....

In partnership with ....

Overall level of independence equates to

....

Night-time extra special care needs

....

'This is me' independence rating runs out on

....

Agreed date for re-assessment

....

Signed .... Signed ....

Level of independence during the night

.... has an overall night-time presentation that has .... extra special care needs. This is because

....

....

....

Extra issues that need taking into consideration

Has a medically controlled breathing problem:

Has asthma	2
Is susceptible to chronic chest infections	2
Warning: This child has allergies!	4
Has no verbal communication	4
Expresses desires and wishes through behaviour	4
Has minor communication difficulties	3
Self-injurious behaviour	4
Attacks others	4
Regularly destroys clothing, soft furnishings, and toys	4

Has epilepsy:

Tonic/Clonic seizures	4
Petit mal seizures	2
Absence seizures	2
At risk from status epilepticus	4

Total night-time extra special care needs equates to ....
Assessed on ....
By ....in partnership with....................

Hello, my name is

....

I was born on

....

I go to school at

....

My key worker and I filled in this form on

....

My book needs updating on...............................

I have an extra special care score of........................

We arrived at this score with the support of

....

My night-time rating is

....

I need to be re-assessed on

....

IMPORTANT INFORMATION ABOUT ME!
(THIS IS CONFIDENTIAL)

Full name:...

Home address:...

....

Next of kin:..

Address and telephone no.:.........................

....

School address/head teacher/class teacher:

....

....

....

Date of birth:...

Name and Address of GP:.............................

....

....Tel..........................

Important medical information:.....................

....

....

Important people in my life: ....

....

This form was filled in by: ....

On:..

Information was given by: ....

....

It needs updating on:....................................

More about me

Ordinary things that happen in my life

Sleeping

Waking up

Personal hygiene

Using the toilet

Eating and drinking

Playing

Going to school

Communicating

Being happy

Being sad

Showing frustration

Being with others

Travelling in a car or mini bus

Being unwell

My favourite things

My bad habits

When I'm out and about

What I know about me

Special information about my health

Admission sheet

Name:..

Arrived today...................at..........via......................

Duration of stay..

Nature of the respite..

....

....

....

In possession of..

....

....

....

Greeted by..

Checked for any cuts and bruises.........................

....

Special information..

....

....

....

....

....

A record of my stay and the care I received

Care plan for..

    Aim

How are we going to do it

When are we going to review it? ....

Who else is to be involved in my care plan?

....

Please fill in daily how much progress I have made towards my aim...
....
....
....
....

Today is my review date. What have you got to say about my care plan?..
....
....
....
....

The Millennium Charter for Children's Health Services

1. All children should have equal access to the best clinical care within a network of services that collaborate with each other.

2. Health services for children and young people should be provided in a child-centred environment separately from adults so that they are made to feel welcome, safe and secure at all times.

3. Parents should be empowered to participate in decisions regarding the treatment and care of their child through a process of clear communication and adequate support.

4. Children should be informed and involved to an extent appropriate to their development and understanding.

5. Children should be cared for at home with the support and practical assistance of community children's nursing services.

6. All staff caring for children shall be specifically trained to understand and respond to their clinical, emotional, developmental and cultural needs.

7. Every hospital admitting children should provide overnight accommodation for parents free of charge.

8. Parents should be encouraged and supported to participate in the care of their child when they are sick.

9. Every child in hospital shall have full opportunity for play, recreation and education.

10. Adolescents will be recognised as having different needs to those of younger children and adults. Health services should therefore be readily available to meet their particular needs.

(Action for Sick Children 1999)

References and Further Reading

Action for Sick Children (1999) *The Millennium Charter for Children's Health Services*. London: Cascade.

Ahmann, E. (1994) 'Family centred care: shifting orientation.' *Pediatric Nursing 20*, 2, 113–117.

Alderman, C. (1998) 'Capital support.' *Nursing Standard 12*, 29, 22–23.

Alderson, P. (2000) *Young Children's Rights: Exploring Beliefs, Principles and Practice*. London: Jessica Kingsley Publishers.

Ashworth, P. (1980) *Care to Communicate*. London: RCN.

Baines, B. (2000) 'Close encounters of slurred kind.' *Nursing Times 96*, 9, 34–35.

Bishop, K.K., Woll, J. and Arango, P. (1993) *Family/Professional Collaboration for Children with Special Health Needs and their Families*. Burlington, VT: Department of Social Work, University of Vermont.

Bowlby, J. (1953) *Childcare and the Growth of Love*. Harmondsworth: Penguin.

Brodin, J. and Paulin, S. (1997) 'Parent's view of respite services for families with children with disabilities in Sweden.' *European Journal of Special Needs Education 12*, 3, 197–208.

Callery, P. and Smith, L. (1991) 'A study of the role negotiation between nurses and the parents of hospitalised children.' *Journal of Advanced Nursing 16*, 772–781.

Campbell, H. (1996) 'Inter-agency assessment of respite care needs of families of children with special needs in Fife.' *Public Health 110*, 151–155.

Cherry, B.S. and Carty, R.M. (1986) 'Changing concepts of childhood in society.' *Pediatric Nursing 12*, 6, 421–424, 460.

Cohen, S. and Warren, R. (1985) *Respite Care: Principles, Programs and Policies*. Austin, Texas: Pro-Ed, Inc.

Cooper, C. (1999) *Continuing Care of Sick Children: Examining the Impact of Chronic Illness*. Salisbury: Quay Books.

Cross, T. (1988) 'Services to minority populations: what does it mean to be a culturally competent professional? Focal point.' *The Bulletin of Research and Training Centre on Family Support and Children's Mental Health. 2*, 4, 1–2.

Darbyshire, P. (1994) *Living with a Sick Child in Hospital: The Experience of Parents and Nurses.* London: Chapman and Hall.

Davies, J. (1996) 'The role of the specialist for families with autistic children.' *Nursing Standard 11*, 3, 36–40.

Day, P.R. (1997) 'Respite care in a children's residential unit: perceptions of parents, young people and staff.' *Social Services Research 2*, 22–36.

Department of Education (1993) *Education Act.* London: HMSO.

Department of Health (1999) *The Government's Objectives for Children's Social Services.* London: HMSO.

Department of Health (2000) *Carers and Disabled Children Act.* Norwich: HMSO.

Duff, G. (1992) 'Respite choice.' *Nursing Times 88*, 33, 65–66.

Erikson, E.H. (1950) *Childhood and Society.* New York: Norton.

Flynn, M., Cotterill, L., Hayes, L. and Sloper, T. (1995) *A Break with Tradition: The Findings of a Survey of Respite Services for Adult Citizens with Learning Disabilities in England.* Manchester: National Development Team.

Folden, S.L. and Coffman, S. (1993) 'Respite care for families of children with disabilities.' *Journal of Pediatric Health Care 7*, 3, 103–110.

Gatford, A. (1999) 'Invisible link.' *Nursing Times 95*, 42, 32–33.

Gravelle, A. (1997) 'Caring for a child with a progressive illness during the complex chronic phase: parents' experience of facing adversity.' *Journal of Advanced Nursing 25*, 4, 738–745.

Hall, S. (1996) 'An exploration of parental perception of the nature and level of support needed to care for their child with special needs.' *Journal of Advanced Nursing 24*, 3, 512–521.

Hewitt, H. (2000) 'Life story books.' *British Journal of Nursing 9*, 2, 90–95.

HMSO (1986) *The Disabled Person's Act.* London: HMSO.

HMSO (1989) *The Children Act.* London: HMSO.

HMSO (1997) *Rights Brought Home: The Human Rights Bill.* London: HMSO.

Hubert, J. (1991) *Home-Bound: Crisis in the Care of Young People with Severe Learning Difficulties: A Story of Twenty Families.* London: King's Fund Centre.

Knafl, K., Breitmayer, B., Gallo, A. and Zoeller, L. (1996) 'Family responses to childhood chronic illness: description of management styles.' *Journal of Pediatric Nursing 11*, 5, 315–326.

Laverty, H. and Reet, M. (2000) 'Model of independence for children with learning disabilities.' *British Journal of Nursing 9*, 19, 2090–2094.

Lyon, C. (1995) 'Helping children with challenging behaviour.' *Nursing Standard 10*, 1, 33–35.

McGill, P. (1996) 'Summer holiday respite provision for the families of children and young people with learning disabilities.' *Child-Care, Health and Development 22*, 3, 203–212.

Mental Health Foundation (1997) *Don't Forget Us: Children with Learning Disabilities and Severe Challenging Behaviour.* London: Mental Health Foundation.

Middleton, L. (1999) *Disabled Children: Challenging Social Exclusion.* Oxford: Blackwell Science.

Millar, N.B. (1994) *Nobody's Perfect: Living and Growing with Children who have Special Needs.* Baltimore: Paul H. Brookes.

Minkes, J., Robinson, C. and Weston, C. (1994) 'Consulting the children: interviews with children using residential respite care services.' *Disability and Society 9*, 1, 47–57.

NHS Executive (1998) *Signposts for Success.* London: HMSO.

O'Brien, J. (1987) 'Discovering community: learning from innovation in services to people with mental retardation.' In R. Kugel (ed) *Changing Patterns in Residential Services for Persons with Mental Retardation.* Washington DC: President's Committee on Mental Retardation.

Olshansky, S. (1972) 'Changing vocational behaviour through normalisation.' In W. Wolfensberger *The Principles of Normalisation in Human Services.* Toronto: National Institute on Mental Retardation.

Oswin, M. (1978) *Children Living in Long-Stay Hospitals.* London: Heinemann Medical (Monograph No. 5).

Oswin, M. (1984) *They Keep Going Away: A Critical Study of Short-Term Residential Care Services for Children who are Mentally Handicapped.* London: King Edward's Hospital Fund for London.

Piaget, J. (1932) *The Moral Judgement of the Child.* London: Routledge and Kegan Paul.

Pickard, J. and Williams, D. (1996) 'Ten things parents of children with learning disabilities want to tell you.' *Journal of the APLD 13*, 3, 16–18.

Pillitteri, A. (1999) *Child Health Nursing Care of the Child and Family.* Philadelphia: Lippincott.

Poyser, J. (2000) 'A framework of care for children with cerebral palsy.' *Nursing Times 96*, 13, 42–44.

Reet, M. (1995) 'Children's nurses' perceptions of their responsibility: a study of change after crisis.' Unpublished MSc dissertation, University of Nottingham.

Robinson, C.A. (1987) 'Roadblock to family centred care when a chronically ill child is hospitalised.' *Maternal-Child Nursing Journal 16*, 3, 181–193.

Roper, N., Logan, W. and Tierney, A. (1983) *Using a Model for Nursing.* Edinburgh: Churchill Livingstone.

Shah, R. (1992) *The Silent Minority Children with Disabilities in Asian Families.* London: The National Children's Bureau.

Sobsey, D. (1999) http://funrsc,fairfield.edu/~jfleitas/dadcope.html Accessed 9 February 2000.

Social Services Inspectorate (SSI) (1998) *Moving into the Mainstream.* London: SSI.

Treneman, M., Corkery, A., Dowdney, L. and Hammond, J. (1997) 'Respite care needs – met and unmet: assessment of needs for children with disability.' *Developmental Medicine and Child Neurology 39*, 8, 548–553.

Vygotsky, L.S. (1978) *Mind in Society.* Cambridge, MA: Harvard University Press.

Whyte, D. (1992) 'A family approach to the care of the child with a chronic illness.' *Journal of Advanced Nursing 17*, 317–327.

Wolfensberger, W. (1972) *The Principles of Normalisation in Human Services.* Toronto: National Institute on Mental Retardation.

Wooley, H., Stein, A., Forrest, G.C. and Baum, J.D. (1989) 'Staff stress and job satisfaction at a children's hospice.' *Archives of Disease in Childhood 64*, 1, 114–118.

Index